**New Directions for
Student Leadership**

Susan R. Komives
EDITOR-IN-CHIEF

Kathy L. Guthrie
ASSOCIATE EDITOR

Leadership Development through Service-Learning

Wendy Wagner
Jennifer M. Pigza
EDITORS

Number 150 • Summer 2016
Jossey-Bass
San Francisco

LEADERSHIP DEVELOPMENT THROUGH SERVICE-LEARNING
Wendy Wagner, Jennifer M. Pigza (eds.)
New Directions for Student Leadership, No. 150, Summer 2016

Susan R. Komives, Editor-in-Chief
Kathy L. Guthrie, Associate Editor

Microfilm copies of issues and articles are available in 16mm and 35mm, as well as microfiche in 105mm, through University Microfilms Inc., 300 North Zeeb Road, Ann Arbor, MI 48106-1346.

New Directions for Student Leadership is indexed in Academic Search Alumni Edition (EBSCO Publishing), Education Index/Abstracts (EBSCO Publishing), ERA: Educational Research Abstracts Online (T&F), ERIC: Educational Resources Information Center (CSC), MLA International Bibliography (MLA).

NEW DIRECTIONS FOR STUDENT LEADERSHIP (ISSN 2373-3349, electronic ISSN 2373-3357) is part of the Jossey-Bass Higher and Adult Education Series and is published quarterly by Wiley Subscription Services, Inc., A Wiley Company, at Jossey-Bass, One Montgomery Street, Suite 1200, San Francisco, CA 94104-4594. POSTMASTER: Send all address changes to New Directions for Student Leadership, Jossey-Bass, One Montgomery Street, Suite 1200, San Francisco, CA 94104-4594.

SUBSCRIPTIONS for print only: $89.00 for individuals in the U.S./Canada/Mexico; $113.00 international. For institutions, agencies, and libraries, $342.00 U.S.; $382.00 Canada/Mexico; $416.00 international. Electronic only: $89.00 for individuals all regions; $342.00 for institutions all regions. Print and electronic: $98.00 for individuals in the U.S., Canada, and Mexico; $122.00 for individuals for the rest of the world; $411.00 for institutions in the U.S.; $451.00 for institutions in Canada and Mexico; $485.00 for institutions for the rest of the world. Prices subject to change. Refer to the order form that appears at the back of most volumes of this journal.

EDITORIAL CORRESPONDENCE should be sent to the Associate Editor, Kathy L. Guthrie, at kguthrie@fsu.edu.

Cover design: Wiley
Cover Images: © Lava 4 images | Shutterstock

www.josseybass.com

CONTENTS

Editors' Notes

This volume is grounded in the fundamental belief that the robust implementation of service-learning in leadership education is a powerful tool to educate students about service and leadership while also contributing to community impact. The complementarity of service-learning pedagogy with leadership education is clear. For example, we find leadership connections to service-learning in:

- The emphasis on building inclusive leadership processes built on trust from the relational leadership model (Komives, Lucas, & McMahon, 2013)
- The collaborative process among individuals, groups, and communities advocated by the social change model of leadership development (Higher Education Research Institution [HERI], 1996; Komives, Wagner, & Associates, 2009)
- The importance of sharing power and expecting personal growth by all parties of transformational leadership (Burns, 1978)
- The ability to discern whether challenges require technical or adaptive solutions from adaptive leadership (Heifitz & Linsky, 2002)

Realizing student learning and community outcomes, however, requires theoretical foundations and intentional design and implementation of service-learning principles.

This volume of *New Directions for Student Leadership* provides both theory and practice to guide service-learning integration into both academic and cocurricular leadership initiatives for high school and college students. The content and examples provided here emphasize how leadership outcomes are enhanced through high-quality application of service-learning. The text is primarily useful for educators and facilitators who want to expand their service-learning expertise and for service-learning educators and facilitators who want to amplify the leadership outcomes of their efforts. Additionally, community leaders in the nonprofit and local government sector who work regularly with student leaders will find this volume to be a useful window into the theory and practice of leadership and service-learning, which will deepen their capacities as coeducators.

New Directions for Student Leadership, no. 150, Summer 2016 © 2016 Wiley Periodicals, Inc., A Wiley Company
Published online in Wiley Online Library (wileyonlinelibrary.com) • DOI: 10.1002/yd.20166

The editors and contributors of this volume operate from a shared conception of service-learning. As a form of experiential learning (Kolb, 1981), service-learning links community service to student learning objectives, includes ongoing reflection, and is grounded in reciprocal community partnerships in which all parties benefit (Jacoby & Associates, 1996). Service-learning can occur in both academic and cocurricular settings, and, the distinction between community service and service-learning is whether or not an experience fulfills the service-learning essentials identified in the definition. Service-learning embedded in leadership education must:

- Specify student learning and development outcomes that link service to academic content.
- Include critical reflection throughout the experience that both challenges and supports students' personal insights, theoretical understandings, and leadership practice.
- Be grounded in reciprocal partnerships with the community, characterized by a primary concern for positive community impact.
- Encourage student leadership as both a process and product of service-learning.
- Engage students and community partners in purposeful action that addresses both immediate and/or systemic change issues.

About This Volume

The chapters in this volume address these five key elements of service-learning by offering both theoretical frameworks and practical advice. The opening chapter, by the volume editors, provides a theoretical orientation to the intersections of the theory and practice of leadership and service-learning. Grounded in a critical perspective, the authors articulate a set of values to guide leadership educators in their service-learning practice.

Chapter 2 by Corey Seemiller, "Complementary Learning Objectives: The Common Competencies of Leadership and Service-Learning," explores the literature on leadership competencies and describes the intersection between the student learning outcomes of service-learning and those competencies. With this knowledge in place, educators can identify which objectives fit their course or program and make intentional choices about the nature of the service-learning projects that will best fit those goals.

Chapter 3, by Julie E. Owen, asserts community engagement creates opportunities for discussion that encourage a critical social justice lens. While engaging students in reflective thinking is not new for leadership educators, service-learning introduces distinct elements to that practice. Potential reflection topics include: the nature and sources of power, who benefits and who is silenced by service and leadership efforts, and the difference between charity and justice. Owen offers practical advice about developmentally sequencing reflective practice.

Developing sustainable community partnerships for service-learning may be a learning area for leadership educators. In Chapter 4, Jennifer M. Pigza focuses on impact-oriented community partnerships that are aimed at long-term engagement rather than stand-alone projects. Here, the POWERful Community Engagement framework—which stands for partnerships, objectives, working, evaluation, and reflection—offers a theory-based practical guide to community partnerships.

With conceptions of learning outcomes, reflection, and community partnerships established, Magali Garcia-Pletsch and Nicholas Longo offer their chapter, "Beyond Tactical Service-Learning: Student Leadership and the Promise of Democratic Engagement," in which they argue for service-learning to reach its democratic potential by unleashing the power of student leadership in a democratic educational process inspired by the Highlander Folk School.

The last three chapters of this volume provide case studies of service-learning in leadership education that engage students and community partners in purposeful action. In Chapter 6, Eric Hartman shares the experience of his two-semester leadership course designed around community-centered and justice-oriented principles. In this example, students are assigned a global issue of injustice and work in teams to develop educational outreach strategies. Through this process, students strengthen their leadership knowledge, clarify their passions, and hone practical skills.

Mentoring is a popular service-learning activity, and in Chapter 7, Lindsay Hastings describes a strengths-based mentoring program designed to create a cascading effect of leadership development: college students mentor youth, who then mentor other youth. The objective for the college students is to identify leadership talents within their mentees, develop their leadership capacities, and direct their developed leadership toward positive reinvestment in others.

The final chapter in this volume is a case study by Vicki Ferrence Ray of the Hugh O'Brian Youth Leadership (HOBY). This leadership development program for high school students is grounded in the social change model of leadership (HERI, 1996) and service-learning methodology. HOBY believes that leadership is action, not title or position, and that no matter a person's age, role, or sector, effective positive leadership is ultimately service to humanity.

Conclusions and Points of Departure

We hope that this volume expands your knowledge about the possibilities and practice of service-learning in leadership education. As you progress through this volume, we encourage you to engage these questions: What social change is required in local, regional, national, and international communities? What kind of leadership does the world demand? What type of service-learning is best reflective of the leadership you espouse?

While the definition of service-learning provides a common ground, it is also a departure point. As Mitchell (2008) has noted, there is a debate in service-learning literature and practice that seems to "divide service-learning into two camps—a traditional approach that emphasizes service without attention to systems of inequality, and a critical approach that is unapologetic in its aim to dismantle structures of injustice" (p. 50). As we editors review the complexity of social issues, the challenges of youth, and the narratives that guide notions of leadership and change, we affirm our belief that a critical approach to leadership and service-learning engenders the development of powerful skills and capacities that can address the systemic social justice issues of our age. This volume provides lessons and guideposts for the journey.

Wendy Wagner
Jennifer M. Pigza
Editors

References

Burns, J. M. (1978). *Leadership*. New York, NY: Harper & Row.

Heifitz, R. A., & Linsky, M. (2002). *Leadership on the line: Staying alive through the dangers of leading*. Boston, MA: Harvard Business Review Press.

Higher Education Research Institute. (1996). *A social change model of leadership development (Version III)*. Los Angeles: University of California Los Angeles, Higher Education Research Institute.

Jacoby, B., & Associates. (1996). *Service-learning in higher education: Concepts and practices*. San Francisco, CA: Jossey-Bass.

Kolb, D. A. (1981). Learning styles and disciplinary differences. In A. W. Chickering & Associates (Eds.), *The modern American college: Responding to the new realities of diverse students and a changing society* (pp. 232–255). San Francisco, CA: Jossey-Bass.

Komives, S. R., Lucas, N., & McMahon, T. R. (2013). *Exploring leadership for college students who want to make a difference* (3rd ed.). San Francisco, CA: Jossey-Bass.

Komives, S. R., Wagner, W., & Associates. (2009). *Leadership for a better world: Understanding the social change model of leadership development*. San Francisco, CA: Jossey-Bass.

Mitchell, T.D. (2008). Traditional vs. critical service-learning: Engaging the literature to differentiate two models. *Michigan Journal of Community Service-Learning, 14*(2), 50–65.

WENDY WAGNER *is the Engaged Faculty Liaison in the Honey W. Nashman Center for Civic Engagement and Public Service and teaches in Human Services & Social Justice at The George Washington University. Wendy is formerly the director of the Center for Leadership and Community Engagement at George Mason University, and founder of the Nonprofit Fellows program and minor. Wendy is a coeditor of* Leadership for a Better World *(2009) and* The Handbook for Student Leadership Programs *(2011), as well as* Exploring Leadership: For College Students Who Want to Make a Difference: Facilitator Activity Guide *(2013) and the accompanying* Student Workbook *(2013). Wendy has a doctorate in college student development from the University of Maryland.*

JENNIFER M. PIGZA *is the director of the Catholic Institute for Lasallian Social Action, the center for service-learning and community engagement at Saint Mary's College of California. She is faculty in Saint Mary's graduate program in leadership and was founding chair of the masters degree in leadership for social justice. Her scholarly interests include critical pedagogy, impact-oriented community partnerships, and institutionalizing community engagement. She is founding coeditor of the journal* Engaging Pedagogies in Catholic Higher Education. *With over 20 years of higher education experience, Jennifer has a doctorate in the social foundations of education from the University of Maryland.*

This chapter provides a theoretical orientation to the intersections of the theory and practice of leadership and service-learning. It articulates a set of values to guide leadership educators in their service-learning practice. The authors advocate a critical approach that fosters social justice.

The Intersectionality of Leadership and Service-Learning: A 21st-Century Perspective

Wendy Wagner, Jennifer M. Pigza

Leadership development involves not just acquisition of content knowledge, but also learning skills and habits of being—learning that is most effectively addressed through experiential learning pedagogies (Cress, Astin, Zimmerman-Oster, & Burkhardt, 2001). Examples of experiential education include internships, field placements, study abroad, active pedagogical activities in the classroom, and service-learning. Service-learning was identified as an excellent context for leadership development as early as 1996 (Higher Education Research Institute [HERI], 1996). More recent research provides empirical evidence that community service experience is a predictor of increased capacity for socially responsible leadership in college students across gender, race, and other demographic groups (Dugan, Kodama, Correia, & Associates, 2013).

Twenty-first century problems require 21st-century notions of leadership and service. The theory and practice of leadership and of service-learning share common elements that make service-learning a fitting pedagogical choice for those who teach and facilitate leadership education in high schools and higher education. While there is consonance, however, the intersectionality of service-learning and leadership also reveals tensions.

- *Intentionality:* Like many of today's leadership development models, such as the relational leadership model (Komives, Lucas, & McMahon, 2013) and the social change model of leadership (HERI, 1996), the intention to contribute to the social good differentiates service-learning from other approaches. However, one person's "good works" is another person's hegemony. Good intentions are not enough to ensure good outcomes (Illich, 1968; McKnight, 1989).

- *Role of Failure:* On occasion, educators discuss the role of allowing failure to create powerful learning moments (Cannon & Edmondson, 2005; Malone, 2015). When students are engaged in a community setting, however, failure means that student learning has come at the expense of a community partner's progress.
- *Participation:* While tasking students with designing a service project provides valuable leadership learning experience, it is unfortunately commonplace for student projects to move from idea to implementation without consulting anyone in the community to be informed by their aspirations, needs, and existing projects. Although many 21st-century leadership models emphasize collaboration and inclusivity, service projects often do not consider community members to be full participants in the group or its leadership processes.
- *Prerequisites of Agency:* The message of today's leadership theories is that anyone can learn to engage in leadership processes (HERI, 1996; Komives et al., 2013). A similar sentiment exists in community service: "Anyone can serve." While this may be well intentioned, it is a false promise that does not recognize the need for learning first. Damage is done in communities when outsiders arrive without proper training for their service activity, an understanding of the social issue at hand, the local history, the ways that power and politics shape the context, and the cultural awareness necessary to be effective in service.
- *Learning Across Cultures:* Many service experiences by their very nature feature opportunities for social perspective taking, conversations across sociopolitical and identity differences, and other experiences identified in the empirical literature as predictors of leadership learning outcomes (Dugan, Bohle, Woelker, & Cooney, 2014; Dugan et al., 2013). However, encouraging student/community member interactions presents an emotional risk for all involved, with a particular risk for community members to be essentialized or stereotyped.

This chapter proposes a set of values to navigate these tensions. The first section of the chapter offers a theoretical context for leadership and service-learning via a review of the schools of thought in each. As a result of this review, we present a framework of shared values present in 21st-century leadership and service-learning theory. Last, the chapter presents closing thoughts and challenges for service-learning and leadership education focused on the pursuit of change.

Schools of Thought in Leadership Studies and Service-Learning

While there are many ways to make meaning of the vast scholarship of both leadership and service-learning, the following section presents the literature in three schools of thought, which have implications for both the study and practice of leadership and service-learning. The review here is representative, not exhaustive. Although the publication dates of the referenced work may suggest a chronological evolution of these ideas, it is important to recognize three things: (1) all three paradigms are present in today's discourse, practice, and scholarship; (2) the influence of power and privilege affects the determination of what ideas are researched and published; and (3) these paradigms have existed in practice and discourse across eras, even if they were not represented in the published literature during certain time periods.

The Functional-Industrial School of Thought.   In leadership studies, the functional-industrial school of thought emerged from the military-industrial context. The Industrial Revolution and two world wars directed research funding to examine the most efficient way to select and train people for positions of leadership (Rost, 1993). Alvesson and Spicer (2012) described this view as the *functional* paradigm, grounded in a positivist epistemology. As such, leadership is considered as an independent construct that can be discovered/understood in an objective, value-neutral way (Alvesson & Spicer), then generalized to other contexts. In this case, the bureaucratic contexts of this research resulted in leadership defined as the traits and behaviors of people in positions of power, and how people in those positions control events and people to achieve their goals. Influence in leader/follower relationships is assumed to flow from the leader, who holds a position of authority, to the followers. Considerations of power are focused on how to obtain it and use it to achieve one's own goals (Alvesson & Spicer, 2012; Rost, 1993). The implication for leadership development then, is self-reflection on which traits, behaviors, or skills (as identified by leadership studies research) one needs to acquire in order to be seen as an effective leader (Northouse, 2015). For example, Zaccaro's (2007) model of leader attributes and leader performance describes attributes such as: social appraisal, problem solving skills, and expertise/tacit knowledge.

Community service has been part of education for over a century and traces its roots to Dewey (1938). The specific concept of service-learning emerged in the mid-20th century (Jacoby & Associates, 1996), and although it did not grow from leadership theory, some orientations to service-learning carry shades of the functional-industrial model. For example, some conceptions of service-learning rely upon an expert model in which a faculty member assume that he or she knows the compelling challenge facing a community and implements a pathway to change. This *noblesse oblige* or deficit-based approach limits or removes community agency and voice, focuses on distinct projects rather than partnerships, provides disproportionate benefits to students and faculty, and assumes that the leader has the skills and traits to diagnose and treat a community problem.

The expression of a leader-centric approach to service-learning may be subtle. For example, the widely used PARE Model of Service (University of Maryland, 2015) offers four steps to service-learning process: preparation, action, reflection, and evaluation. The first step, preparation, includes preparing students regarding logistics, expectations, learning goals, and issue and community orientation—all of which are essential practices. By beginning with preparation, however, the model does not provide guidance about how the service site is identified, how to develop partnerships, or who is engaged in the process. Without such guidance, a leader-centric approach may prevail.

The Postindustrial/Relational School of Thought.   As a political scientist and biographer of several U.S. presidents, James MacGregor Burns (1978) became convinced that a leadership paradigm grounded in hierarchical contexts and transactional relationships did not produce theory that fits the leadership experiences he chronicled. Rather, he observed that leaders and followers influence each other and the outcomes of leadership included meeting goals and also the personal development of those involved. By the 1990s, a paradigm shift in leadership thinking had been identified (Rost, 1993), which was a better fit in the so-called *knowledge era*, than the assumed bureaucratic context of the industrial paradigm (Alvesson & Spicer, 2012). The postindustrial leadership paradigm (Rost, 1993) reflects a context in which new ideas, innovation, and creativity are the important shared aims among collaborators who may or may not be doing their work within hierarchical structures or formal organizations (Uhl-Bien, Marion, & McKelvey, 2007).

In this school of thought, leadership is not the trait of the person who has authority, but the interactive, dynamic process between people who collaborate in an interdependent way (Komives et al., 2013; Rost, 1993; Uhl-Bien et al., 2007). Collectively identified goals are the ideal and questions of power are related to identifying processes that empower everyone in the shared effort to contribute their perspectives and skills. Influence is important, but is thought to occur through the building of trust and relationships rather than through chains of command (Rost, 1993; Uhl-Bien et al., 2007). The implications for leadership development are the need to develop awareness of one's values and commitments and the ability to be collaborative with others who are honoring their values and commitments (HERI, 1996).

This paradigm is *interpretive* in epistemology (Alvesson & Spicer, 2012; Kezar, Carducci, & Contreras-McGavin, 2006; Komives & Dugan, 2010; Uhl-Bien & Ospina, 2012), in which knowledge is seen as socially constructed. Rather than an objective, generalizable list of skills or traits, leadership is understood as a process of shared-meaning making. Describing complexity theory, a theory representative of this paradigm, Uhl-Bien et al. (2007) described leadership as a dynamic that is socially constructed in context, "a context in which patterns over time must be considered and where history matters" (p. 299). It is through the meaning-making process that the group collectively creates how leadership will be defined and practiced in that space.

The context of leadership in this paradigm expands to civic spaces and leadership for social change (HERI, 1996), increasing the need to examine how change is influenced. While the military and industrial contexts may assume control and step-by-step standardization, scholars like Margaret Wheatley (2006) introduced a nonlinear/networked way of understanding how change happens in a system into the mainstream leadership literature. This view holds that the many parts of a system are all linked, such that change in one part of the system will have an impact in other parts, in ways that may or may not be predictable. Leading change requires attention to shifting realities and coordinated nudges of influence throughout the system.

Most service-learning theory and practice resides in this socially constructed framework grounded in relationship. For example, while the PARE Model begins with the preparation of students for service, the OPERA Model (Welch, 2010) of service-learning begins with the identification of objectives for both student learning and community development, and then proceeds to explore partnerships, engagement, reflection, and assessment. Pigza (2016) takes this further in her POWERful model. It begins with a campus-community partnership that then evolves into the development of objectives for student learning and development and community impact, and continues process with working, evaluation, and reflection (also see Chapter 4). Further emphasizing a relational orientation, Enos and Morton (2003) ground their model of partnership development in relational leadership models and advocate that service-learning partnerships move from being transactional to transformational in nature.

Emerging Critical Perspectives.   Critical perspectives in leadership theory examine power and the ways that existing leadership models and practice reinforce the privilege of dominant social groups (Alvesson & Spicer, 2012; Dugan, in press; Kezar et al., 2006). In recent years, the intersection of critical theory and leadership studies has challenged the field to acknowledge the pervasiveness of dominant identities, norms, and values, including White, masculine, straight, and Christian ways of being, in forming the "right" ways of being as leaders (Bordas, 2012; Dugan, in press).

Critical perspectives on leadership call for *critical judgment* when engaging in leadership processes. This means recognizing and questioning deeply held assumptions: that leadership is good, that authority is bad, or that leadership is even needed at all (Alvesson & Spicer, 2012). Those exercising leadership, regardless of position, need to learn to critically evaluate their dynamics to formulate their own most empowering ways of making a collective change effort. The implications for leadership development are the need to be reflective about what history and leadership experiences can reveal about one's unconscious biases and unacknowledged privilege in order to engage with others in more just and equity processes of leadership.

Freire's *Pedagogy of the Oppressed* (2014/1968) is a frequent reference point for service-learning educators drawn to the critical framework where knowledge is grounded in experience and where action in the world coupled with reflection can bring about social change. In critical pedagogy, questions of power are at the center; this also holds true in critical service-learning. Rhoads (1997) connected the ideas of critical pedagogy to service-learning, introducing the term critical service-learning. Butin (2007) expanded on that work, proposing that service-learning can be justice-oriented if educators and facilitators embrace the notion of the contingency of truth, if the design compels an investigation of taken-for-granted knowledge, and if it rejects binary thinking about problems and solutions in favor of complexity. At a practical level, for example, this critical shift requires that long-term community impact and development are the core purposes of service-learning (Stoecker, Loving, Reddy, & Bollig, 2010) rather than the learning and development of students. One of service-learning's most vocal advocates of a critical perspective is Mitchell (2008). In order to develop a critical perspective, she suggests that service-learning must:

- Promote social justice over other forms of citizenship
- Challenge the structures that create the conditions that require service as a response
- Name the way that power is experienced in the service relationship and works to address inequities
- Address the key social issues of contemporary life
- Expand research to assess progress toward social justice aims, long-term community development, and learning and development outcomes for students from underrepresented groups

This discussion of the three paradigms of thought related to the theory and practice of leadership and service-learning, compels advocates of critical pedagogical approaches (such as ourselves) to state foundational values to guide the inclusion of service-learning in leadership courses and programs. While the functional-industrial and postindustrial/relational schools of thought can benefit both student learning and communities, we believe that the complexity of students, of their learning environments, and of contemporary social problems requires a critical perspective.

Critical Values for Service-Learning in Leadership Development

The notion of foundational principles to guide practice is common in service-learning and experiential education. For example, Sigmon (1979) proposed three principles of service-learning and Koliba, O'Meara, and Seidel (2000) proposed 39 social justice principles for experiential education. Grounded in a critical perspective of the intersection of leadership and service-learning described above, we present six values that serve as the foundation for 21st-century leadership and service-learning endeavors.

Awareness of Context.   The value of understanding context emerges from the assumption that "situatedness" matters. In the case of service-learning in leadership development, the relevance of individual and group identity, cultural context, community history and politics, and cultural humility are all part of the "situatedness." The leadership learning outcomes for a particular course or program are also important contexts.

Reciprocal Participation.   Critical scholarship in both leadership and service-learning emphasizes equal participation, shared power, and reciprocal relationships rather than influence, resources, and knowledge that flow from dominant to subordinate groups. A critical perspective promotes leadership as a process among people who all have influence on each other and has a radical welcoming posture to the wisdom and knowledge within marginalized groups. Service is no longer considered an opportunity for students to "practice" their skills in underprivileged communities, rather, the people in the community should be considered contributing group members.

Critical Examination of Power and Privilege.   Contemporary leadership studies acknowledge the benefit of a diversity of perspectives and the need to create an organizational culture in which everyone is empowered to question the group's purposes and processes. Today's leaders need to cultivate critical judgment in themselves and others in order to foster multicultural group processes that reflect group members' diverse ways of being. Justice-oriented service-learning maintains an interrogation of power and privilege throughout the process.

Reflective Practice.   Current approaches to leadership development and service-learning heavily emphasize the role of reflection in enhancing self-awareness, and meaning-making through reflection is the cornerstone to transformational learning. The development of a reflective practice provides a foundation for lifelong learning about content, process, self, and the world, and serves as an assessment of whether one's actions are congruent with the values and intent for the community. Leadership courses and programs must include intentionally designed and multimethod reflection components.

Sustained Engagement.   The value of sustained engagement emphasizes sustainability in several ways. Grounded in a notion of relational leadership, sustained engagement indicates an ongoing relationship with a community organization, neighborhood, or group of residents to create change. Sustained engagement also implies the desire that students, faculty, and facilitators develop an ongoing engagement with a social issue that is personally compelling. And finally, sustained engagement refers to the potential ability for community organizations to continue new initiatives that may be created through a service-learning and leadership program.

NEW DIRECTIONS FOR STUDENT LEADERSHIP • DOI: 10.1002/yd

Commitment to Change and Justice. The final foundational value that emerged from the literature review is the belief and commitment to change and justice. The goal is not to engage for the sake of leadership development only, but to contribute to a positive difference being made. Local change should be designed to meet immediate needs, build community capacity, and influence systems to address the root causes of social problems.

The values presented here are not practical steps to designing and implementing service-learning in leadership courses and programs. The remaining chapters in this book offer such guidance. Rather, the values represent an orientation that informs the practical work. For example, the values do not mention evaluation and assessment, although these are key elements of service-learning. Educators and facilitators would ask themselves: How do each of these values influence evaluation and assessment? And, the values do not indicate what activities are acceptable for service-learning. Rather, educators would ask: How do these values influence how service activities are designed? Table 1.1 offers a summary of these values and proposes questions that educators and students can ask themselves before, during, and after a service-learning in leadership course or program.

A New Tension Emerges: Critical Congruence

This chapter begins with the identification of several tensions that emerge in the intersections of leadership development and service-learning. The tensions included those of intentionality, failure, participation, the prerequisites of agency, and learning across cultures. The discussion of literature and exploration of values provide guidance and context for negotiating these tensions. A critical perspective on the foundational values of service-learning in leadership courses and programs reveals an additional tension: *critical congruence*. This tension reveals questions:

- Can today's leadership education programs partner with organizations and communities who operate from paradigms inconsistent with 21st- century leadership and critical perspectives?
- Do leadership programs only partner with like-minded groups and individuals?
- What role do leadership development programs have in influencing the values orientation of community entities?
- How might a justice-oriented organization positively influence the values and practices of leadership development programs?

It is perhaps this final tension that is the most challenging of all the tensions, because it operates at a meta level. For example, imagine a collaboration between an educational institution and several nonprofits. They have agreed to the collective impact model (Kania & Kramer, 2011) to

Table 1.1   Service-Learning and Leadership: A Reflection on Values

Value	Guiding Questions
Awareness of Context	What is the leadership context and content that informs the service experience? What is the history and context of the community and/or organization where we serve? What policies and politics influence the issue or concern? What does it mean to practice cultural humility?
Reciprocal Participation	How can this project ensure that community partners and community members are engaged in the design and delivery of service? What specific practices encourage deep listening of all group members? Who is missing from pertinent conversations? In what ways can assessment and evaluation be inclusive of multiple perspectives? How do we support the participation of community members?
Critical Examination of Power and Privilege	How are the knowledge and wisdom in community partners and community members valued equally to the knowledge and wisdom from higher education? How does my own social location (and that of my group) impact how I (we) enter community? How do students of dominant identities and subordinate identities experience service and leadership?
Reflective Practice	How is reflection integrated into the entire arc of the service-learning experience? In what ways does this course or program encourage life-long habits of personal meaning-making and ongoing transformation? How does reflection challenge and support students' personal insights, theoretical understandings, and leadership practice?
Sustained Engagement	How can my leadership course or program be engaged over the long term with a community and/or organization? Can the projects or programs that we work on be sustained by the community after this course or project is complete? How might students be engaged in this issue beyond this initial commitment?
Commitment to Change and Justice	What does social change mean to me, our group/class, the organization where we are serving, and the people being served? How does the manner in which I practice leadership and service represent a justice orientation? How does this course or program model reciprocal partnerships, characterized by a primary concern for positive community impact?

develop long-term community change. What is revealed through time, however, is that one of the organization directors operates rather strictly from a functional-industrial perspective, which does not match the collective impact process, and at a practical level is making progress difficult. The partnership cannot be successful without a more involved critical approach, but the director is slow to evolve his thinking and practice. How does the partnership proceed amidst this tension of critical congruence?

Leaders, educators, community workers, and change agents are human beings and human organizations in process. While there may be occasions when a highly critically grounded leadership program pairs with a critically grounded community agency, the likelihood is that both parties will be imperfect in their practice. In these moments, remembering that social justice is both a process and a product provides a container for this tension.

In Closing

> The work of the world is common as mud.
> Botched, it smears the hands, crumbles to dust.
> But the thing worth doing well done
> has a shape that satisfies, clean and evident.
> (from "To Be of Use," Piercy, 1982)

As practice-oriented scholars and scholarly oriented practitioners, we believe strongly in the purposes, principles and practices of service-learning and leadership education grounded in a critical perspective. The inherent tensions and opportunities that emerge at the intersection of leadership and service-learning require a wide-awake orientation on behalf of faculty, facilitators, students, and community collaborators. This collective wide-awake orientation enables us to engage in the real work of justice and community development. It is work that is common, worth doing, and satisfies.

References

Alvesson, M., & Spicer, A. (2012). Critical leadership studies: The case for critical performativity. *Human Relations, 65*, 367–390.

Bordas, J. (2012). *Salsa, soul, and spirit: Leadership for a multicultural age* (2nd ed.). San Francisco, CA: Berrett-Koehler.

Burns, J. M. (1978). *Leadership*. New York, NY: Harper & Row.

Butin, D. W. (2007). Justice-learning: Service-learning as justice-oriented education. *Equity & Excellence in Education, 40*, 177–183.

Cannon, M. D., & Edmondson, A. C. (2005). Failing to learn and learning to fail (intelligently): How great organizations put failure to work to innovate and improve. *Organizational Failure, 38*, 299–319.

Cress, C. M., Astin, H. S., Zimmerman-Oster, K., & Burkhardt, J. C. (2001). Developmental outcomes of college students' involvement in leadership activities. *Journal of College Student Development, 42*, 15–27.

Dewey, J. (1938/1951). *Experience and education*. New York, NY: Macmillan.

Dugan, J. P. (in press). *Leadership theory: Cultivating critical perspectives*. San Francisco, CA: Jossey-Bass.

Dugan, J. P., Bohle, C. W., Woelker, L. R., & Cooney, M. A. (2014). The role of social perspective-taking in developing students' leadership capacities. *Journal of Student Affairs Research and Practice, 51*, 1–15.

Dugan, J. P., Kodama, C., Correia, C., & Associates. (2013). *Multi-institutional study of leadership insight report: Leadership program delivery.* College Park, MD: National Clearinghouse for Leadership Programs.

Enos, S., & Morton, K. (2003). Developing a theory and practice of campus-community partnerships. In B. Jacoby (Ed.), *Building partnerships for service-learning* (pp. 20–41). San Francisco, CA: Jossey-Bass.

Freire, P. (2014/1968). *Pedagogy of the oppressed* (30th anniversary edition). New York, NY: Bloomsbury.

Higher Education Research Institute. (1996). *A social change model of leadership development (Version III).* Los Angeles: University of California–Los Angeles, Higher Education Research Institute.

Illich, I. (1968). To hell with good intentions. In *An address to the Conference on Inter-American Student Projects (CIASP) in Cuernavaca, Mexico, on April* (Vol. 20). Retrieved from http://www.wmich.edu/sites/default/files/attachments/u5/2013/To%20Hell%20with%20Good%20Intentions.pdf

Jacoby, B., & Associates. (1996). *Service-learning in higher education: Concepts and practices.* San Francisco, CA: Jossey-Bass.

Kania, J., & Kramer, M. (2011, Winter). Collective impact. *Stanford Social Innovation Review,* 36–41.

Kezar, A. J., Carducci, R., & Contreras-McGavin, M. (2006). Rethinking the "L" word in higher education: The revolution of research on leadership. *ASHE Higher Education Report, 31*(6). New York, NY: Jossey-Bass.

Koliba, C., O'Meara, K., & Seidel, R. (2000). Social justice principles in experiential education. *NSEE Quarterly, 2000, 26*(1), 1 & 27–29.

Komives, S. R., & Dugan, J. P. (2010). Contemporary leadership theories. In R. Couto, *Political and civic leadership: A reference handbook* (pp. 111–120). Thousand Oaks, CA: Sage.

Komives, S. R., Lucas, N., & McMahon, T. R. (2013). *Exploring leadership: For college students who want to make a difference* (3rd ed.). San Francisco, CA: Jossey-Bass.

Malone, D. (2015, April 27). *Productive failure: The value of letting students fail.* Retrieved from http://www.wherelearningclicks.com/productive-failure-the-value-of-letting-students-fail/

McKnight, J. (1989). *Why servanthood is bad.* Retrieved from http://mn.gov/mnddc/mcKnight/documents/Why_Servanthood_is_Bad.pdf

Mitchell, T. D. (2008, Spring). Traditional vs. critical service-learning: Engaging the literature to differentiate two models. *Michigan Journal of Community Service-Learning,* 50–65.

Northouse, P. G. (2015). *Leadership: Theory and practice* (7th ed.). Los Angeles, CA: Sage.

Piercy, M. (1982). To be of use. *Circles on the water: Selected poems of Marge Piercy* (p. 106). New York, NY: Knopf.

Pigza, J. M. (2016). The POWER model: Five core elements for teaching community-based research. In M. Beckman & J. F. Long (Eds.), *Community-based research: Teaching for community impact* (pp. 93–107). Sterling, VA: Stylus.

Rhoads, R. A. (1997). *Community service and higher learning: Explorations of the caring self.* Albany: State University of New York Press.

Rost, J. C. (1993). *Leadership for the twenty-first century.* Westport, CT: Greenwood.

Sigmon, R. (1979). Service-learning: Three principles. *Synergist, 8,* 9–11.

Stoecker, R., Loving, K., Reddy, M., & Bollig, N. (2010). Can community-based research guide service-learning? *Journal of Community Practice, 18,* 280–296.

Uhl-Bien, M., Marion, R., & McKelvey, B. (2007). Complexity leadership theory: Shifting leadership from the industrial age to the knowledge era. *The Leadership Quarterly, 18,* 298–318.

Uhl-Bien, M., & Ospina, S. (2012). *Advancing relational leadership research: A dialogue among perspectives*. Charlotte, NC: Information Age.

University of Maryland. (2015). http://thestamp.umd.edu/leadership_community_service-learning/academic_opportunities/faculty_service-learning/designing_quality_service-learning_courses

Welch, M. J. (2010). O.P.E.R.A.: A first letter mnemonic and rubric for conceptualising and implementing service learning. *Issues in Educational Research, 20*, 76–82.

Wheatley, M. J. (2006). *Leadership and the new science: Discovering order in a chaotic world* (3rd ed.). San Francisco, CA: Berrett-Koehler.

Zaccaro, S. J. (2007). Trait-based perspectives of leadership. *The American Psychologist, 62*, 6–16; 43–47.

WENDY WAGNER *is the Engaged Faculty Liaison for The Honey W. Nashman Center for Civic Engagement and Public Service and faculty member of human services & social justice at George Washington University.*

JENNIFER M. PIGZA *is the director of the Catholic Institute for Lasallian Social Action and graduate faculty member for the MA and EdD in Leadership at Saint Mary's College of California.*

NEW DIRECTIONS FOR STUDENT LEADERSHIP • DOI: 10.1002/yd

2

This chapter provides a framework for intentionally designing service-learning experiences that contribute to leadership competency development of students. Assessment of leadership competency development is also addressed.

Complementary Learning Objectives: The Common Competencies of Leadership and Service-Learning

Corey Seemiller

The evidence is clear that students can experience transformational learning and development through well-designed service-learning (Eyler, Giles, Stenson, & Gray, 2001). Given the connection between leadership development and social change (Pigza, 2015), it is no surprise that this learning and development includes enhancing competencies related to leadership.

Although service-learning has been the topic of much research, there is little scholarship on how to design service-learning experiences that result in intentional development, and even less on leadership development specifically. One way to explore the intentionality of service-learning for leadership development is by connecting with the literature on leadership competencies. This chapter will provide a framework for intentionally designing service-learning experiences that contribute to leadership competency development of students.

Overview of Leadership Competencies

Leadership competencies are knowledge, values, abilities, and behaviors that contribute to someone successfully completing a role or task (Seemiller, 2013b). Competencies are general and categorical, while outcomes are the specific basis for assessment. Any one leadership competency may be evidenced by multiple outcomes. For example, analysis is a leadership competency that can be associated with specific outcomes, such as a student's

New Directions for Student Leadership, no. 150, Summer 2016 © 2016 Wiley Periodicals, Inc., A Wiley Company
Published online in Wiley Online Library (wileyonlinelibrary.com) • DOI: 10.1002/yd.20168

assessment of varying policy approaches to a social issue or a group's ability to apply theory to their analysis of a case study.

The competencies referenced in this chapter are from the student leadership competencies model, derived from a study that began with the examination of contemporary leadership models and frameworks in higher education in an effort to uncover embedded leadership competencies. The models and frameworks used included the relational leadership model (Komives, Lucas, & McMahon, 2013), social change model of leadership development (Higher Education Research Institute [HERI], 1996), exemplary leadership practices (Kouzes & Posner, 1995), The Council for the Advancement of Standards in Higher Education's standard on student leadership (Dean, 2006), and *Learning Reconsidered* (Day et al., 2004).

From this analysis, an initial list of leadership competencies was compiled and then cross-referenced with the learning outcomes of 522 academic programs within all 97 academic program-accrediting agencies in higher education to confirm and refine the initial list. What resulted is a list of 60 leadership competencies, each with four dimensions: knowledge, value, ability, and behavior (Seemiller, 2013b). These student leadership competencies were selected as a framework for this chapter due to their universality across collegiate academic disciplines and their widespread use in curricular and cocurricular programs in higher education.

Leadership Competencies and Service-Learning Program Design

Although service-learning is a useful pedagogy for the development of leadership competencies, it is less clear to what extent this development is coincidental or a result of intentional choices and design. The following five steps provide this chapter's framework for service-learning program design using a leadership competency-based approach.

1. *Select the leadership competencies:* Identify the leadership competencies you want students to learn and develop.
2. *Select an appropriate form of service-learning:* The service experience should align with the learning goals.
3. *Consult with community partner(s):* Work with local organizations or community leaders to identify projects that would build their capacity or meet an existing need.
4. *Action and reflection:* Engage with students and community partners in the service-learning experience while embedding reflection throughout.
5. *Assess:* Assess students' leadership competency learning and development, and assess the community benefit and impact.

The remainder of this chapter explores this five-step process.

Select Leadership Competencies

The student leadership competencies comprise 60 competencies across eight conceptual categories including: learning and reasoning; self-awareness and development; group dynamics; interpersonal interaction; civic responsibility; communication; strategic planning; and personal behavior (Seemiller, 2013b).

In selecting competencies for student leadership development, it is important to narrow the list of 60 to those competencies most critical to the purpose of the experience. Selection of the competencies should be based on the educator's understanding of students' learning needs and the learning objectives of a course, program, or experience. Leadership development programs benefit from clearly articulated mission statements, which then guide decisions about which leadership competencies are most desired.

In some cases, the leadership development experience is woven into the learning goals of an academic discipline. In these cases, the leadership competencies selected should align with those identified by that academic program. To find out which leadership competencies are associated with particular academic programs, Jossey-Bass hosts the free Student Leadership Competencies Database that lists every accredited academic program in higher education and the leadership competencies necessary for graduates of those programs (Seemiller, 2013a). For example, industrial engineering requires graduates to have the leadership competencies of creating change and idea generation (Seemiller, 2013a). Knowing this may make the process easier in selecting which competencies to focus on for the service-learning experience in an industrial engineering course.

Select an Appropriate Form of Service-Learning

Service-learning can be defined as "the various pedagogies that link community service and academic study so that each strengthens the other" (Ehrlich, 1996, as cited in Felten & Clayton, 2011, p. 75), and it can be integrated into academic and cocurricular settings (Jacoby, 1996). Through service-learning, students of leadership have invaluable exposure to the complexities of working collaboratively with people to address social change goals in a way that is inclusive of multiple perspectives, approaches, and priorities. Service-learning can provide opportunities to see how change is influenced, by working with others in teams and through coalition-building across communities. It can also be a powerful experience through which students come to understand the reach and impact of social inequities, and explore the pathways leaders take to create more just communities.

What then do students learn and develop through service-learning? In this author's review of more than 70 service-learning studies, 30 of the 60 student leadership competencies result from service-learning experiences.

NEW DIRECTIONS FOR STUDENT LEADERSHIP • DOI: 10.1002/yd

Ample research has been conducted to highlight the learning-outcomes of service-learning, but few studies have disaggregated the particular learning outcomes of specific forms of service experiences. Scholars agree that service-learning is conceptually and pragmatically diverse (Butin, 2007; Deans, 1999; Westheimer & Kahne, 2004 as cited in Boyle-Baise et al., 2006). So, in addition to the 30 leadership competencies generally associated with service-learning, each form of service is associated with leadership competencies specific to that experience. The forms of service discussed in this chapter are reflective of the *Pathways of Public Service* from the Stanford University Haas Center for Public Service (Haas Center for Public Service, n.d.). The Pathways of Public Service represent distinct yet interdependent ways to create social change. Table 2.1 expands on the Stanford's pathways, suggesting several subcategories within pathways such as direct service and community engaged learning and research.

Table 2.1 is not exhaustive, as it highlights only competencies embedded into outcomes that were measured in the studies reviewed. Lack of measurement, however, does not mean that a competency is not linked to a particular service experience. So, it is important to supplement this list with competencies that could be related to the particular service experience. For example, although it is not listed in the table, it is fair intuitively to suppose that organizing a philanthropy campaign would be associated with the competencies of communication and persuasion. Therefore, leadership educators should use this framework as a starting point and then augment with additional intended competencies based on the specific expectations built into the service-learning experience.

Consult With Community Partners

Unlike most other learning experiences within higher education, service-learning involves careful consideration of how reciprocity benefits student learning and community goal attainment. Community partners have an insider perspective on the issue being addressed and their goals for community change and development. For example, if a community partner requests direct service, but the instructor wants to create an action research project, there is a mismatch. Instructors and community partners must work in collaboration to align service-learning activities with leadership learning objectives. It is important to incorporate the partner's feedback in identifying the roles students can play and the leadership competencies that may be associated with the experience.

Service-learning is also unique in that it engages community partners, such as staff or clients at a nonprofit, in coeducator roles. Because community partners are involved directly on site and may have more exposure to students than the instructor or program coordinator, the role of community partner as coeducator is vital to the process of student leadership development. Thus, it is critical to collaborate with community partners

Table 2.1 Public Service Pathways and Associated Leadership Competencies

Form of Service	Definition	Project Examples	Associated Student Leadership Competencies (Seemiller, 2013b)
Direct Service: Short-Term Service Project	Giving personal time, energy, or resources to address immediate community needs or priorities. Short-term service projects in which the issue addressed often continues to persist long after the service.	Reading to children, cleaning up a park, planting trees, making art with hospital patients, or staffing a community event.	Personal contributions, creating change, problem solving, synthesis, empathy, empowerment, service (Fenzel & Leary, 1997), self-understanding, self-development, confidence, appropriate interaction, diversity, social responsibility (Simons & Cleary, 2006), scope of competence, idea generation (Sedlak, Doheny, Panthofer, & Anaya, 2003), conflict negotiation, others' circumstances (Astin & Sax, 1998).
Direct Service: Ongoing Community Involvement	Formal, long-term role or position with a cause or agency.	Serving as a youth mentor, being a tutor, being an active member of a community association.	Appropriate interaction, problem solving, functioning independently, and decision-making (Brennan & Barnett, 2009; Brennan, Barnett, & Lesmeister, 2007, as cited in Brennan & Barnett, 2009).
Community Engaged Learning and Research: Action Research	Applying learning to inform action on community issues through research projects conducted in and with the community. (Elden & Chisholm, 1993, and Shanks et al., 1993, both as cited in McKay & Marshall, 2001).	Collecting data through focus groups, interviews, and surveys, as well as researching best practices or cases to share with a community agency.	Collaboration, problem solving, research, and social responsibility (Reardon, 1998).

(Continued)

Table 2.1 Continued

Form of Service	Definition	Project Examples	Associated Student Leadership Competencies (Seemiller, 2013b)
Community Engaged Learning and Research: Case Study	Applying learning to inform action on community issues through team-based projects that apply disciplinary knowledge and skills to provide ideas/solutions.	Class assignments that culminate in a paper or presentation, or team competitions in which a community partner selects a winner with the most feasible idea.	Analysis, evaluation, problem solving (Ekachai, 2002, as cited in Johnson, Judge, & Wanless, 2013), collaboration, verbal communication, writing (Maier-Lytle et al., 2010, as cited in Johnson, Judge, & Wanless, 2013), confidence (Carter, 1995; Clawson & Haskins, 2006; Corey, 1998; Garvin, 2003; Maier-Lytle et al., 2010; Smith et al., 2005; Tillman, 1995; all as cited in Johnson, Judge, & Wanless, 2013).
Community Engaged Learning and Research: Skills-Based Project	Applying learning to inform action on community issues by combining students' disciplinary knowledge and skills with community-members' intimate understanding of local issues to design a process or product.	Computer science students creating a mobile application that enhances childhood literacy, architecture/design students optimizing shared space in the design of a community center, accounting students providing assistance with tax forms to low-income families, or education students planning and implementing new math-based afterschool curriculum.	Verbal communication, idea generation, and collaboration (Carlson & Sullivan, 2005).
Advocacy Project	Taking action to educate and persuade decision-makers in order to influence the implementation of policies, and practices that benefit the common good.	Informing and giving feedback to public officials or corporate leaders on the ramifications of their policies, implementing social media campaigns to create pressure for certain decisions, organizing collective action such as boycotting.	Confidence, advocating for a point of view (Berke, 2010), diversity, empowerment, systems thinking (Quaye, 2007).

(Continued)

Table 2.1 Continued

Form of Service	Definition	Project Examples	Associated Student Leadership Competencies (Seemiller; 2013b)
Education Project	Formal and informal processes aimed to educate others about a social issue.	Community writing, film or art projects, presentations/trainings, and information distribution.	Advocating for a point of view, confidence, systems thinking (Murray, Pope, & Rowell, 2010).
Political Involvement	Participating in processes of democratic self-governance in order to influence positive community change.	Canvassing for candidates, getting signatures for ballot initiatives, persuading others to vote, informing the public about ballot initiatives.	Service (Freyss, 2003), analysis, evaluation, idea generation, research, and problem solving (Goodhart et al., 2006).
Philanthropy	Activities taken to raise funds to support community organizations or initiatives.	Planning and implementing fundraising events, conducting fundraising campaigns such as GoFundMe, raising public awareness of issues to persuade them to financially support a cause or organization.	More research is needed in this area.
Social Entrepreneurship	Social entrepreneurship: Creating or expanding market-oriented solutions to a community problem for a triple-bottom line project mission: financially, environmentally, and socially sustainable.	Running a coffee shop on campus that serves only fair-trade coffee, starting up a computer recycling program that refurbishes and sells computers at a reduced cost to the community, meeting with local business leaders to assist them in redesigning their business plan to incorporate a social mission.	Helping others, positive attitude (Hoffman, 1999, as cited in Beck, 2005), idea generation (Smith et. al., 2006, as cited in Hytti, Stenholm, Heinonen, & Seikkula-Leino, 2010).

to ensure that the competencies selected are embedded into the service-learning experience from the community partner's perspective. With this agreement in place, all parties need a clear understanding of their role in the service-learning experience. (Chapter 4, "Community Partnerships," provides more details about developing and sustaining impact-oriented relationships with community partners.)

Action and Reflection

In this fourth step of service-learning, students are engaged in intentionally designed service-learning projects and reflecting on that experience in light of the leadership competencies and outcomes of a course or program. (Chapter 3, "Fostering Critical Reflection," offers extensive guidance about the frequency, format, and framework of reflection.)

Assess Student Development in Leadership Competencies

In terms of service-learning, assessment refers to assessment of student learning and development, as well as assessment of community benefit and community impact. While this chapter is focused on the assessment of student learning and development, educators should engage in a community assessment as well. Assessment of student learning and development should occur throughout the service-learning experience and leadership course or program. Using a leadership competency-based approach both in curricular and cocurricular service-learning moves assessment away from measuring what students learned in general to measuring the extent to which they learned what was intended.

There are many benefits to using a leadership competency-based approach when assessing service-learning. First, having a common language of this student leadership competencies model that showcases what students learn through service-learning makes comparing data more seamless. Using a universal set of leadership competencies provides the opportunity for service-learning program benchmarking as well as benchmarking with other leadership development initiatives across campus that may use the student leadership competencies model as a framework. Second, the use of a competency-based framework in assessment helps educators more clearly make the case that their programs contribute to leadership development. It helps align the leadership and service-learning programs with both civic learning goals (National Task Force on Civic Learning and Democratic Engagement, & Association of American Colleges and Universities, 2012) and career preparation (National Association of Colleges and Employers, 2014).

To effectively do assessment using a competency-based framework, it is important to account for the learning dimensionality. Each leadership competency has four dimensions: knowledge, value, ability, and behavior (Seemiller, 2013b). Fortunately, these dimensions align strikingly well with the learning dimensions identified in the service-learning literature. Hatcher and Steinberg (2007) advocate measuring the dimensions of knowledge, skills, and dispositions related to civic outcomes (as cited in Bringle & Hatcher, 2009). One can also consider the alignment between the four dimensions of the student leadership competencies model (Seemiller, 2013b) and Eyler and Giles' (1999) lenses of service-learning:

1. Knowledge: "I know what I ought to do and why."
2. Value: "I ought to do."
3. Ability: "I know how to do."
4. Behavior: "I must and will do."

Consider what competency might be developed through a particular service-learning experience, and further, what dimension. For example, understanding how to address a social issue reflects the knowledge dimension, whereas believing it to be an important issue to address reflects the value dimension. The ability dimension refers to developing the skills and capacities needed to address the issue, while behavior focuses on a person's actual engagement in a particular competency during a service experience. Employing measurements that address dimensions will help uncover the nuances of student learning and development. Four approaches to assess service learning competency development are in Table 2.2.

Considerations

There are some considerations to take into account when using a competency-based approach for service-learning. First, how might competency development truly and accurately be measured? Short-term engagement can be challenging to measure as the experience may not have been long enough in duration to make an impact on leadership development. On the other hand, longer-term projects may have too many intervening variables that cannot be controlled, making it difficult to discern whether it was the project or another factor that influenced leadership development. To mitigate these issues, consider using multiple forms of assessment as well as longitudinal assessment methods to get a greater and more accurate picture of student leadership development.

Another factor to consider is that experiences like service-learning may provide opportunities to shift attitudes, open perspectives, create passions, and transform students, which may not readily be captured through solely using a competency-based approach. And, as competencies are inherently leader-centric focusing on the individual leader, using this approach may not take into account process-oriented models of leadership that reflect a group working together towards change. It is important to consider that using a competency-based approach only provides one lens to assess service-learning gains in students. However, there are many other important factors

Table 2.2   Approaches to Assessment of Leadership Competencies

1. Utilize any pre-set scales, assessments, or validated instruments related to the intended competencies. For example, if conflict negotiation is an intended competency, it could be beneficial to use an existing conflict scale that has been previously tested.
2. Use the self-reported evaluation measurements available on the Jossey-Bass website (Seemiller, 2013a) for measuring Student Leadership Competencies. These measurements are available by each dimension of each competency. For example, below are the measurements for social responsibility for each dimension (Seemiller, 2013a):
   1. Knowledge: As a result of participating in this service experience, my understanding of social responsibility (did not increase, slightly increased, moderately increased, greatly increased).
   2. Value: As a result of participating in this service experience, the value I place on social responsibility (did not increase, slightly increased, moderately increased, greatly increased).
   3. Ability: As a result of participating in this service experience, my motivation to act socially responsible (did not increase, slightly increased, moderately increased, greatly increased).
   4. Behavior: During this service experience, (I did not, I did to some extent, I did) act socially responsible.
3. Create reflection questions that allow for examples of learning and development to emerge. Then, look for themes related to intended competencies and dimensions of learning. For example: What was your greatest learning through this service experience? In addition, asking a question related to a particular competency as a pre- and post- can provide insight on the growth of one's value related to the selected competency. For example, consider the following question as a prereflection and postreflection question: What is the value of social responsibility to a community?
4. Ask community partners to evaluate the perceived competency development of students who participated in service-learning. This is recommended only for projects that involve few students, are longer-term, and in which the student has a connection to the evaluator so that the feedback is useful. Being able to involve the community partner from the onset in being aware of the intended competencies, suggesting additional associated competencies, and ensuring the pedagogy is a match will provide the foundation that effectively involves the community partner in the assessment phase.

that can result from service-learning that should be captured through other methods.

The competencies that emerged related to service-learning from these studies may not necessarily be universal or replicable. Factors such as the structure, length of time, and depth of the experience; the effectiveness of learning and reflection tied to the experience; and the validity of the assessment measures all play a role in what can be determined in regard to students' competency development through service-learning. Thus, it is important to consider this framework as a tool for guiding intentional design and measurement and not a steadfast assurance of what students will learn.

Finally, student competency development is not the only aim of service-learning; service-learning is also about contributing to the community in positive ways. Service-learning is a mutually beneficial process that allows students to learn while addressing a real community issue. If at any time service-learning becomes lopsided and moves more toward learning or service, then the essence of service-learning subsides. So, in designing experiences focused on competency development, ensure that the experiences also advance community goals.

Conclusion

Students' participation in service-learning can result in the development of leadership competencies. But, it is important to be mindful of intentionally designing experiences rather than simply integrating service-learning because it is generally beneficial. By selecting pedagogies that are associated with intended competencies and integrating assessment methods that fit with the contextual factors of the experience, educators can offer meaningful, yet intentional, contributions to student leadership development.

References

Astin, A. W., & Sax, L. J. (1998). How undergraduates are affected by service participation. *Journal of College Student Development, 39*, 251–263.

Beck, E. (2005). The UCSD student-run free clinic project: Transdisciplinary health professional education. *Journal of Healthcare for the Poor and Underserved, 16*, 207–219.

Berke, D. L. (2010). Advocacy as service-learning. *Family Science Review, 15*(1), 13–30.

Boyle-Baise, M., Brown, R., Hsu, M., Jones, D., Prakash, A., Rausch, M., ... Wahlquist, Z. (2006). Learning service or service-learning: Enabling the civic. *International Journal of Teaching and Learning in Higher Education, 18*, 17–26.

Brennan, M. A., & Barnett, R. V. (2009) Bridging community and youth development: Exploring theory, research, and application. *Community Development, 40*, 305–310.

Bringle, R. G., & Hatcher, J. A. (2009). Innovative practices in service-learning and curricular engagement. In L. R. Sandmann, C. H. Thornton, & A. J. Jaeger (Eds.), *New Directions for Higher Education: No. 147. Institutionalizing community engagement in higher education: The first wave of Carnegie classified institutions* (pp. 37–46). San Francisco, CA: Jossey-Bass.

Butin, D. W. (2007). Justice-learning: Service-learning as justice-oriented education. *Equity & Excellence in Education, 40*, 177–183.

Carlson, L. E., & Sullivan, J. F. (2005). Bridging the gap between invention and innovation. *International Journal of Engineering Education, 21*, 205–211.

Day, P., Dungy, G. J., Evans, N., Fried, J., Keeling, R., Komives, S. R., ... Salvador, S. (2004). *Learning reconsidered: A campus-wide focus on the student experience.* Washington, DC: National Association of Student Personnel Administrators and American College Personnel Association.

Dean, L. A. (Ed.). (2006). *CAS professional standards for higher education* (6th ed.). Washington, DC: Council for the Advancement of Standards in Higher Education.

Deans, T. (1999). Service-learning in two keys: Paulo Freire's critical pedagogy in relation to John Dewey's pragmatism. *Michigan Journal of Community Service Learning, 6*, 15–29.

Eyler, J. S., & Giles, D. E. (1999). *Where's the learning in service-learning?* San Francisco, CA: Jossey-Bass.

Eyler, J. S., Giles, D. E., Stenson, C. M., & Gray, C. J. (2001). At a glance: What we know about the effects of service-learning on college students, faculty, institutions, and communities, 1993–2000: Third edition. *Higher Education. Paper 139.* Retrieved from http://digitalcommons.unomaha.edu/slcehighered/139

Felten, P., & Clayton, P. H. (2011). Service-learning. In W. Buskist & J. E. Groccia (Eds.), *New Directions for Teaching and Learning: No. 128. Evidence-based teaching* (pp. 75–84). San Francisco: Jossey-Bass.

Fenzel, L. M., & Leary, T. P. (1997). *Evaluating outcomes of service-learning courses at a parochial college.* Paper presented at the annual meeting of the American Educational Research Association, Chicago, IL.

Freyss, S. F. (2003). *Learning political engagement from the experts: Advocacy groups, neighborhood councils, and constituency service.* Paper presented at the Annual Meeting of the American Political Science Association, Philadelphia, PA.

Goodhart, F. W., Hsu, J., Baek, J. H., Coleman, A. L., Maresca, F. M., & Miller, M. B. (2006). A view through a different lens: Photovoice as a tool for student advocacy. *Journal of American College Health, 55*(1), 53–56.

Haas Center for Public Service. (n.d.). *Pathways of public service.* Retrieved from https://haas.stanford.edu/about/mission-and-principles/pathways-public-service

Higher Education Research Institute (HERI). (1996). *A social change model of leadership development (Version III).* Los Angeles, CA: University of California Los Angeles, Higher Education Research Institute.

Hytti, U., Stenholm, P., Heinonen, J., & Seikkula-Leino, J. (2010). Perceived learning outcomes in entrepreneurship education. *Education & Training, 52,* 587–606.

Jacoby, B. (1996). *Service-learning in higher education: Concepts and practices.* San Francisco, CA: Jossey-Bass.

Johnson, J. E., Judge, L. W., & Wanless, E. (2013). Using a case study competition as an intense learning experience in sport management. *Sport Management Education Journal, 7,* 34–42.

Komives, S. R., Lucas, N., & McMahon, T. (2013). *Exploring leadership: For college students who want to make a difference* (3rd ed.). San Francisco, CA: Jossey-Bass.

Kouzes, J. M., & Posner, B. Z. (1995). *The leadership challenge* (2nd ed.). San Francisco, CA: Jossey-Bass.

McKay, J., & Marshall, P. (2001). The dual imperatives of action research. *Information Technology & People, 14*(1), 46–59. http://doi.org/10.1108/09593840110384771

Murray, C. E., Pope, A. L., & Rowell, P. C. (2010). Promoting counseling students' advocacy competencies through service-learning. *Journal for Social Action in Counseling and Psychology, 2*(2), 29–47.

National Association of Colleges and Employers. (2014). *The skills/qualities employers want in new college graduate hires.* Retrieved from http://www.naceweb.org/about-us/press/class-2015-skills-qualities-employers-want.aspx

National Task Force on Civic Learning and Democratic Engagement, & Association of American Colleges and Universities. (2012). *A crucible moment: College learning & democracy's future, a national call to action.* Washington, DC: Association of American Colleges and Universities.

Pigza, J. M. (2015). Navigating leadership complexity through critical, creative, and practical thinking. In J. E. Owen (Ed.), *New Directions in Student Leadership: No. 145. Innovative learning for leadership development* (pp. 35–48). San Francisco, CA: Jossey-Bass.

Quaye, S. J. (2007). Hope and learning: The outcomes of contemporary student activism. *About Campus, 12*(2), 2–9.

Reardon, K. M. (1998). Participatory action research as service-learning. In R. A. Rhoades & J. P. F. Howard (Eds.), *New Directions for Teaching and Learning: No. 73. Academic service learning: A pedagogy of action and reflection* (pp. 57–64). San Francisco, CA: Jossey-Bass.

Sedlak, C. A., Doheny, M. O., Panthofer, N., & Anaya, E. (2003). Critical thinking in students' service-learning experiences. *College Teaching, 51*(3), 99–103.

Seemiller, C. (2013a). *Jossey-Bass student leadership competencies database.* Retrieved from http://www.wiley.com/WileyCDA/Section/id-818224.html

Seemiller, C. (2013b). *The student leadership competencies guidebook.* San Francisco, CA: Jossey-Bass.

Simons, L., & Cleary, B. (2006). The influence of service-learning on students' personal and social development. *College Teaching, 54*(4), 307–319.

COREY SEEMILLER is an assistant professor of leadership studies in education and organizations at Wright State University.

3

This chapter explores how community engagement creates opportunities to facilitate meaningful discussions about issues including: the nature and sources of power; who benefits and who is silenced by service and leadership efforts; which community actions result in change rather than charity; and how to developmentally sequence reflective practice.

Fostering Critical Reflection: Moving From a Service to a Social Justice Paradigm

Julie E. Owen

Adopting a learning outlook and growth mindset seems to be a key differentiator between leaders who attempt to motivate followers through the use of rewards and corrective action, and those who view their role as building collective capacity for meaningful change. Much has been written on the intersections of leadership and learning (Daloz Parks, 2005; Owen, 2015; Preskill & Brookfield, 2009; Roberts, 2007) and indeed learning is core to modern approaches to leadership such as transformational, servant, relational, and adaptive theories. This capacity to learn from experiences is tied directly to one's ability to analyze, integrate, and interrogate those experiences in light of existing knowledge and schemas.

Reflection, intentionally pausing to carefully consider aspects of an experience, is an essential component of learning, yet is often short-changed in formal leadership education, especially in Western contexts. Meanwhile, the field of community service-learning has long embraced the concept of reflective practice as a core element of pedagogy and practice (Eyler, Giles, & Schmiede, 1996; Rice, 2010; Schoen, 1983, 1987). This chapter will explore ways leadership educators can integrate practices of reflection, especially of deep or critical reflection, in order to more effectively foster leadership for social change.

New Directions for Student Leadership, no. 150, Summer 2016 © 2016 Wiley Periodicals, Inc., A Wiley Company
Published online in Wiley Online Library (wileyonlinelibrary.com) • DOI: 10.1002/yd.20169

Distinguishing Among Levels of Reflection

Reflection is not a new concept. Dewey (1933) defined reflection as "the active, persistent, and careful consideration of any belief of or supposed form of knowledge in the light of the grounds that support it" (p. 6). There are numerous prescriptions on how to best engage in reflection, and a variety of differences among concepts of personal reflection, common sense reflection (Moon, 2004), and reflection in action (Schoen, 1983). More recently, scholars and practitioners have concluded that not all reflection is equally efficacious, and indeed, shallow or merely descriptive reflection, especially as tied to service-learning, can be damaging (Butin, 2006; Mitchell, 2008). Jacoby (2014) describes these dangers: "experience without critical reflection [described below] can all too easily allow students to reinforce their stereotypes about people who are different from themselves, develop simplistic solutions to complex problems, and generalize inaccurately based on limited data" (p. 26). These cautions are not limited to service-learning. It is easy to see how students engaged in leading change or leading for innovation could also fall prey to similar parochial thinking.

Most service and community-based learning programs now differentiate the processes of reflection from those of *critical* reflection. Jacoby (2014) defines the latter: "Critical reflection is the process of analyzing, reconsidering, and questioning one's experiences within a broad context of issues and content knowledge" (p. 26); it guides students into a depth of thinking that challenges underlying assumptions and beliefs. Eyler, Giles, and Schmeide (1996) offer that critical reflection should be conducted in a way that is continuous, connected, challenging, and contextualized. That is, critical reflection should take place before, throughout, and after a community engagement experience (continuous); should serve as a bridge between the action or experience and more cognitive or discipline-based ways of knowing (connected); should involve being pushed out of one's comfort zones to make connections and think in new ways (challenging); and should be framed in appropriate ways given the context of the experience (contextualized) (Collier & Williams, 2005). Mitchell (2008) describes how a commitment to critical reflection shifts the emphasis of service-learning from individual actors to systems thinking:

> While individual change and student development are desired outcomes of traditional and critical service-learning, critical service-learning pedagogy balances the student outcomes with an emphasis on social change. This requires rethinking the types of service activities in which students are engaged, as well as organizing projects and assignments that challenge students to investigate and understand the root causes of social problems and the courses of action necessary to challenge and change the structures that perpetuate those problems. (p. 53)

In addition to these hallmarks of critical reflective practice, there are often political dimensions as well. Kreber (2012) states that "an important feature that distinguishes critical reflection from these other constructs is its strong foundation in critical theory [for example Freire, 1970; Habermas, 1971; Gramsci, 1971] and variations enriched by postmodern ideas [Brookfield, 1995, 2000; Tierney & Rhoads, 1993]" (p. 324). Critical reflection demands that experiences and issues be examined in light of social and political forces, link explicitly to further social action, and reveal hegemonic ideology—that is, the influence of unquestioned dominant cultures and philosophies. Freire (1970) did not believe that reflection and action could be separated. He coined the concept of *praxis*, or action and reflection upon the world in order to change it. Through critical or deep reflection, assumptions about the world can be revealed and interrogated, power dynamics and relationships can be examined, and diverse and often contradictory worldviews can be tested. While there are elements of critical thinking in critical reflection, critical thinking as typically defined is often considered a politically neutral enterprise that involves applying logic to a problem or situation.

Critical reflection goes beyond critical thinking in several ways. In addressing issues of the nature and sources of power, for example, critical reflection asks students to consider who is represented in the staffing and leadership of an organization, and who is enacting formal and informal power. Critical reflection invites students to consider who benefits and who is silenced by service and leadership efforts. For example, students can explore whether guests or clients of an organization have a voice in setting an organization's goals or programmatic priorities. Critical reflection also draws distinctions between acts of charity and acts of social change. Students can be asked to consider whether their own community actions support social change or provide immediate relief (and the potential benefits of both types of action). Finally, through critical reflection students are encouraged to know and discuss the systemic and institutionalized nature of oppression. By asking a series of "why" questions, students may develop a more complex understanding of the social issue evidenced in their service.

Table 3.1 offers sample reflection questions by level of criticality. Note how questions move from simple didactic retelling of events from a monolithic perspective to those where students "become constructive critics of themselves, society, politics, and course content" (Pigza, 2010, p. 75). Deeper levels of critical reflection offer more complex analyses of multiple contexts, perspectives, and diverse constructions of meaning.

Connecting Critical Reflection to Leadership Education and Development

So what can leadership educators learn from service-learning's approach to critical reflection? Kreber (2012) cites research that critical reflection is

Table 3.1   Sample Reflection Questions by Level of Critical Reflection

Levels of Critical Reflection	Sample Reflective Questions
Surface (descriptive):	
• Focuses on singular aspect of a situation or experience • Uses unexamined and unsupported personal beliefs as evidence • May acknowledge different perspectives without valuing or discriminating among them • Lists facts learned, places visited, tasks completed	• What happened? • What did we do today? • What did you see, hear, smell, touch, say? • What is a moment that stands out for you? • What surprised you? Frustrated you? Confused you? Disappointed you? Angered you? • How did this affect you?
Emerging (analysis and application):	
• Reflection provides a cogent critique from a single perspective, but may fail to see the broader system in which the issue or situation is embedded and other factors that may make change difficult to achieve. • May make some connections to the issue or discipline, but the connections may not be deep or insightful. • Demonstrates a beginning ability to interpret evidence and draw reasonable conclusions.	• What are you learning from this? • What do you understand differently now? • What are the strengths and limitations of this service experience? • How does this relate to larger contexts, theories, ideas? • What social issues are connected to the problem addressed by the service experience? • What will you do with what you have learned?
Deep (synthesis and critique):	
• Participants view situations from several perspectives, demonstrate clarity of reasoning, and place their experiences in broader, nuanced, and complex contexts. • Perceive conflicting goals and choices of individuals involved in a situation and acknowledge that differences in ideas or choices can be analyzed and evaluated. • Recognize that decisions and actions are situationally dependent. Can examine own responsibility and connection to issues at hand.	• What influence does culture have on this interaction? • What influence does power have on this interaction? • How does your understanding of service impact this interaction? • What voices are missing from the conversation? • What current systems maintain the problem and how can they be addressed? • How have my own assumptions been challenged through this experience?

Source: Adapted from Bradley (1995); Collier and Williams (2005); Owen and Wagner (2010); Pigza (2010); Preskill and Brookfield (2009); Rice (2010).

essential to sustaining positive personal relationships; productivity, decision-making, and well-being in the workplace; personal meaning making; and to fostering a healthy democracy. Each of these aims are also connected to the goals of leadership education, especially those of collaborative and postindustrial approaches to leadership.

The Multi-Institutional Study of Leadership (MSL) identified community service as one of the strongest predictors of socially responsible leadership (Dugan, Kodama, Correia, & Associates, 2013). The authors describe that if community service experiences are to leverage leadership learning most effectively then "the quality with which the experience is processed is of equal importance" (p. 12). Participants are more likely to gain leadership outcomes from service-learning when:

- Service experiences are designed such that students work with individuals and communities as opposed to working on behalf of them
- The nature of the service experience parallels the values of the type of leadership being cultivated
- Critical reflection is incorporated as a tool for students to interrogate their personal values and challenge normative assumptions
- Students explicitly process service experiences in the context of leadership
- Students examine what additional leadership knowledge and skills are necessary to sustain difficult and complex work

In many ways, critical reflection is the bridge that allows learners to connect their community service experiences to leadership-related themes such as developing critical group-related skills, deepening personal commitments to shared public problems, building resilience for working in complex systems to create change, and disrupting assumptions about social systems and how they operate (Eyler & Giles, 1999; Vogelgesang & Astin, 2000).

Moving From Critical Reflection to Critical Discourse and Action: Three Applications

Developing more complex and interdependent ways to view the world are important but not sufficient levers for social change. Creating lasting change requires actively working to address root causes of issues, to redistribute power, and to develop deep, reciprocal, and authentic relationships (Mitchell, 2008; Morton, 1995). Kasl and Yorks' (2012) model of holistic epistemology includes the concept of presentational knowing, which is "a way of knowing that fosters transformative learning in both individuals and larger human systems by connecting thinking to feeling, thus providing the 'flow in between' that enriches practical action" (p. 504). Presentational knowing links experiential knowing (which comes from "*being in*

Table 3.2   Building Coherence and Human Connection through Presentational Knowing

Levels of Presentational Knowing	Experiential Knowing (derives from being in the world)	Propositional Knowing (involves reflecting on the world)
Intrapersonal/Holistic Knowing Brings feelings and emotions into consciousness.	Affective feeling and emotion	Critical reflection
Interpersonal/Relational Knowing Dialogue across differences challenges taken for granted worldviews and builds empathy for lived experiences of others.	Empathic field	Critical discourse
Collective/Systems Learning Creates spaces for conversations about community's group identity and place within society, and, builds solidarity for action.	Group identity	Community reflection and dialogue for action

Source: Adapted from Kasl and Yorks' (2012) Model of Holistic Epistemology.

the world") and propositional knowing (which comes from "*reflecting on the world*") (p. 516). Because presentational knowing connects experiences and reflection across three levels—intrapersonal or holistic knowing, interpersonal or relational knowing, and collective or systemic knowing—it is an apt frame for the types of knowing that emerge through service and critical reflection.

Table 3.2 depicts Kasl and Yorks' (2012) model of holistic epistemology and describes the three levels of presentational knowing and how they result from the interplay between experiential knowing and propositional knowing. Internal coherence and human connection are fostered by engaging in all three types of knowing. The three ensuing examples can be adapted by leadership educators as ways to interrogate existing systems and structures and an individual's role in challenging or sustaining those structures in a connected and caring way.

Critical Reflection (Intrapersonal): Addressing the Disorienting Dilemma. Service-learning and leadership educators understand that learning requires change and change only occurs when complacency and one's typical worldview are challenged. Many service-learning efforts "confront participants with the unexpected, unfamiliar, surprising, and perhaps even disturbing, thereby calling into question the suppositions they hold and possibly revealing them as distorted" (Kreber, 2012, p. 330).

Critical reflection is most likely to happen among students when they face a disorienting dilemma, then work to make meaning of the dilemma.

Mezirow (2000) outlined 10 phases of perspective transformation. Table 3.3 offers an example of a student encountering an unexpected obstacle in his desire to help the community and how that individual worked through the stages of perspective transformation in order to arrive at a more complex understanding of asset-based approaches to change. Educators will see connections between this model and diverse learning and development theories (Baxter Magolda, 1992; Kohlberg, 1976; Kolb, 1984; Perry, 1970).

Critical Discourse (Interpersonal): Short-Term Immersion Experiences Enhance Understanding across Differences. Critical discourse, or dialoguing across differences, is essential for enhancing understanding and building empathy. Many service-learning practitioners have developed skills in facilitating inter-group dialogue and cross-cultural reflection as part of the evolution of alternative breaks and other service-immersion programs. Leadership educators, though perhaps just as likely to work with students across cultural contexts, may not have as frequent access to resources and experiences that develop skills in facilitating critical discourse.

Kiely (2004, 2005) conducted a longitudinal case study examining the ways an international alternative break service-learning program contributed to the development of transformative learning. A grounded theory inquiry process revealed five stages of perspective transformation as outlined in Table 3.4.

Kiely's findings, augmented by Jones et al. (2012), reveal the transformative potential of short-term immersion experiences, such as service-learning, and link much of this transformation to the power of critical discourse. Border crossing often "elicited in students a scrutiny of their own identities, backgrounds, and privileges in relation to those with whom they were interacting, and a breaking down of stereotypes" (pp. 215–216) leading participants to try and close the gap between themselves and others by identifying elements of common humanity. The more students spent time interacting across cultures and experiences, the more they developed a shared connection and commitment to further actions.

Much of the service-learning literature describes this action of "dialogic engagement" as critical to developing authentic relationships and sharing power. Mitchell (2008) describes the importance:

> A critical service-learning pedagogy asks everyone to approach the service-learning relationship with authenticity. In this process, we would develop a shared agenda, acknowledge the power relations implicit in our interactions, and recognize the complexity of identity—understanding that our relationship within the service-learning context is further complicated by societal expectations. (p. 10)

Community Reflection and Dialogue for Action: The Highlander Experience. Perhaps the most complex level of critical reflection is conducting reflection on a systems level and using dialogue as a springboard

NEW DIRECTIONS FOR STUDENT LEADERSHIP • DOI: 10.1002/yd

Table 3.3   Ten Phases of Perspective Transformation

Phase and Service-Learning Example

1. Experiencing an event in society that disorients one's sense of self within a familiar role.
   A student organization has a member who works at a bakery where day-old bagels are thrown out every evening. The student takes the bagels to a local food pantry and asks that they be donated to feed the homeless. The food pantry rejects the donation of the bagels as many of their clients have inadequate access to dental care and the stale bagels frequently cause dental issues. The student feels affronted that the donation was not welcome.

2. Engaging in reflection and self-reflection.
   The student relates this story to a member of the service-learning office on campus. The service-learning practitioner asks the student what assumptions he made as he decided on the donation. The student reflects on the assumption that food-insecure individuals would be glad to have any food, and not question the condition of the food. The student also reflects that he didn't think about possible dental issues related to poverty.

3. Critically assessing personal assumptions and feelings.
   The student realizes his own privileged access to health care blinded him to the fact that not everyone has equal access. He also hadn't considered the fact that their donations could be burdensome or even harmful to the people they were trying to help.

4. Relating discontent to similar experiences of others; recognizing shared problems.
   The student reflects that perhaps this experience was like when all his peers assumed his parents paid for his college tuition, when in fact he was paying his own way through college.

5. Identifying new ways of acting.
   The student decides to think more critically and carefully in engaging in acts of charity in the future. He decides there is value in letting the community state what their needs are rather than assuming he knows what they are.

6. Building personal confidence and competence.
   The student realizes this is a new way of thinking about the community for him and shares his new understanding of asset-based approaches to change with the rest of the student organization members.

7. Planning a new course of action.
   The organization decides they still want to work with the food pantry and reaches out to ask how their help could be most beneficial.

8. Acquiring knowledge and skills necessary to implement this new course of action.
   The food pantry requests that the student group agree to fill a regular shift helping distribute donations from 11 a.m. to 1 p.m. every Friday. They also talk to the students about getting support for an addendum to the county budget that increase funding for human services.

9. Trying out the planned action and assessing the results.
   The student organization commits to this plan and develops a sustained relationship with both the food pantry staff, as well as several regular clients who make use of the food pantry services. They work on campus and in the community to raise awareness about the upcoming vote on the budget addendum and share stories of the hard-working clients and families they met during their work at the shelter.

10. Reintegrating into society with new role behaviors, new assumptions, and perspectives.
    The students work to promote this service opportunity to other student groups in order to fill more shifts at the pantry, and decide to develop a policy watch program that advocates in long term ways for increased support for human service agencies on the local, state, and national level. Their visibility on these issues also invites food insecure students from their own campus to visit the group to discuss developing a food pantry for students in need.

Source: Adapted from Cranton (2002); Mezirow (1991).

Table 3.4   Stages of Transformative Learning through International Service-Learning

Stage	Student Actions
Contextualized Border Crossing	Examines how personal, structural, historical, and programmatic elements of the context for service-learning frame the unique nature and impact of the experience.
Dissonance	Experiences disconnect between their own personal context and that of the immersion service-learning experience.
Personalizing	Builds relationships with community members which allow them to humanize previously abstract ideas such as poverty.
Processing	Intellectually engages with the experience and challenges previously held assumptions.
Connecting	Develops affective connections with community members and commits to work for justice upon return to their home culture and contexts.

Source: Adapted from Jones et al. (2012); Kiely (2004; 2005).

for action. Beyond mere personal reflection, or discussions within a group or organization, community dialogue and reflection transgresses organizational and contextual boundaries in order to invite shared understanding and commitment to action. Drawing on Buber's (1958) concept of dialogic moments, these conversations reflect on moments of dissonance within a community. Pearce (2001) describes that "the defining characteristic of dialogic communication is when people are able to hold their own position and 'allow others to hold theirs by being profoundly open to hearing others' positions without needing to oppose or assimilate them" (p. 11). The four conditions of transformative dialogue in groups include a shared commitment and motivation to learn; curiosity and openness to difference; emotional engagement through storytelling; and using inquiry as a catalyst for refection and mutual meaning making (MacKeracher, 2012).

The Highlander Folk School, also known as the Highlander Research and Education Center, provides an example of this notion of community reflection that leads to action. The Highlander Research and Education Center:

> Serves as a catalyst for grassroots organizing and movement building in Appalachia and the South. We work with people fighting for justice, equality and sustainability, supporting their efforts to take collective action to shape their own destiny. Through popular education, participatory research, and cultural work, we help create spaces—at Highlander and in local communities—where people gain knowledge, hope and courage, expanding their ideas of what is possible. (Highlander Research and Education Center, 2015)

Myles Horton, the director of Highlander (Adams, 1975) from 1932 until the early 1980s, knew that increased understanding "is best achieved through participation in an actual situation, and that conflict and crisis must be seized as opportunities for people to learn how they can effectively resolve their own individual and community problems" (Preskill & Brookfield, 2009, p. 119). For example, Highlander hosted a gathering of a diverse group of people in response to the *Brown v. Board of Education* decision which called for the integration of public schools. After extensive storytelling and context sharing, the group "began the task of analyzing the information by asking questions, searching out contradictions, looking for sources of strength, and considering starting points for bringing about change" (p. 121). This process valued personal story, openness to learning, courageous questions, and commitment to further action.

This form of community reflection linked to specific action planning connects to Freire's concept of *praxis*, or action and reflection in order to change the world. In what ways can leadership educators and service-learning practitioners alike invite students and community members to come together around shared public problems and engage in deliberative dialogue to deepen understanding and commitment to change?

Reflection for Transformation

As stated previously, engaging students in reflective thinking to facilitate learning from experience is not a new concept for leadership educators, however, there is much to be gained by gleaning insights from the reflective practice of service-learning practitioners. This chapter explored the ways community engagement creates opportunities to facilitate meaningful discussions about issues including: the nature and sources of power; who really benefits and who is silenced by service and leadership efforts; which community actions result in change rather than charity; and how to developmentally sequence reflective practice across increasingly complex ways of knowing. The power of linking leadership and critical reflection augments the transformative potential of leadership efforts—for individuals, groups, and communities. Stephen Brookfield (1995) offers sage advice: "it becomes easy to lose sight of the political underpinnings, dimensions, and consequences of our reflection. But how we reflect and what we chose to reflect on are partisan questions. . . . Reflection in and of itself is not enough; it must always be linked to how the world can be changed." (p. 217).

References

Adams, F. (1975). *Unearthing seeds of fire: The idea of Highlander.* Winston-Salem, NC: Blair.

Baxter Magolda, M. (1992). *Knowing and reasoning in college: Gender related patterns in students' intellectual development.* San Francisco, CA: Jossey-Bass.

Brookfield, S. D. (1995). *Becoming a critically reflective teacher*. San Francisco, CA: Jossey-Bass.

Brookfield, S. D. (2000). Transformative learning as ideology critique. In J. Mezirow & Associates (Eds.), *Learning as transformation: Critical perspectives on a theory in process* (pp. 125–150). San Francisco, CA: Jossey-Bass.

Buber, M. (1958). *I and thou*. New York, NY: T&T Clark.

Butin, D. W. (2006). The limits of service learning in higher education. *The Review of Higher Education, 29*(4), 473–498.

Collier, P. J., & Williams, D. R. (2005). Reflection in action. In C. R. Cress, P. J. Collier, V. L. Reitenauer (Eds.), *Learning through serving: A student guidebook for service-learning across the disciplines* (pp. 83–97). Sterling, VA: Stylus.

Cranton, P. (2002). Teaching for transformation. In J. M. Ross-Gordon (Ed.), *New Directions for Adult and Continuing Education: No. 93. Special issue: Contemporary viewpoints on teaching adults effectively* (pp. 63–72). San Francisco, CA: Jossey-Bass.

Daloz Parks, S. (2005). *Leadership can be taught*. Boston, MA: Harvard Business School Press.

Dewey, J. (1933). *How we think: A restatement of the relation of reflective thinking to the educative process*. Lexington, MA: Heath.

Dugan, J. P., Kodama, C., Correia, B., & Associates. (2013). *Multi-institutional study of leadership insight report: Leadership program delivery*. College Park, MD: National Clearinghouse for Leadership Programs.

Eyler J., Giles D. E., & Schmiede (1996). *A practitioner's guide to reflection in service-learning: Student voices and reflections*. Corporation for National Service. Nashville, TN: Vanderbilt University.

Eyler, J., & Giles, D. E. (1999). *Where's the learning in service-learning?* San Francisco, CA: Jossey-Bass.

Freire, P. (1970). *Pedagogy of the oppressed*. New York, NY: Continuum.

Gramsci, A. (1971). *Selection from the prison notebooks*. London, England: Lawrence and Wishart.

Highlander Research and Education Center (2015). *Mission*. Retrieved from http:// highlandercenter.org/about-us/mission/

Habermas, J. (1971). *Knowledge and human interests*. Boston, MA: Beacon Press.

Jacoby, B. (2014). *Service-learning essentials: Questions, answers, and lessons learned*. San Francisco, CA: Jossey-Bass.

Jones, S. R., Rowan-Kenyon, H. T., Ireland, S. M., Niehaus, E., & Skendall, K. C. (2012). The meaning students make as participants in short-term immersion programs. *Journal of College Student Development, 53*(2), 201–220.

Kasl, E., & Yorks, L. (2012). Learning to be what we know: The pivotal role of presentational knowing in transformative learning. In E. W. Taylor & P. Cranton (Eds.), *The handbook of transformative learning* (pp. 503–519). San Francisco, CA: Jossey-Bass.

Kiely, R. (2004). A chameleon with a complex: Searching for transformation in international service-learning. *Michigan Journal of Community Service-Learning, 10*(2), 5–20.

Kiely, R. (2005). A transformative learning model for service-learning: A longitudinal case study. *Michigan Journal of Community Service-Learning, 12*(1), 5–22.

Kohlberg, L. (1976). Moral stages and moralization: The cognitive-developmental approach. In T. Lickona (Ed.), *Moral development and behavior* (pp. 31–53). New York, NY: Holt.

Kolb, D.A. (1984). *Experiential learning: Experience as the source of learning and development*. Englewood Cliffs, NJ: Prentice Hall.

Kreber, C. (2012). Critical reflection and transformative learning. In E. W. Taylor & P. Cranton (Eds.), *The handbook of transformative learning* (pp. 323–341). San Francisco, CA: Jossey-Bass.

MacKeracher, D. (2012). The role of experience in transformative learning. In E. W. Taylor & P. Cranton (Eds.), *The handbook of transformative learning* (pp. 342–354). San Francisco, CA: Jossey-Bass.

Mezirow, J. (1991). *Transformative dimensions in adult learning.* San Francisco, CA: Jossey-Bass.

Mezirow, J. (2000). *Learning as transformation: Critical perspectives on a theory in progress.* San Francisco, CA: Jossey-Bass.

Mitchell, T. D. (2008). Traditional vs. critical service-learning: Engaging the literature to differentiate two models. *Michigan Journal of Community Service Learning, 14*(2), 50–65.

Moon, J. A. (2004). *A handbook of reflective and experiential learning.* New York, NY: RoutledgeFalmer.

Morton, K. (1995). The irony of service: Charity, project, and social change in service-learning. *Michigan Journal of Service-Learning, 2*(1), 19–32.

Owen, J. E. (Ed.). (2015). *New Directions for Student Leadership: No 1. Innovative learning for leadership development.* San Francisco, CA: Jossey-Bass.

Owen. J. E., & Wagner, W. (2010). Situating service-learning in the context of civic engagement. In B. Jacoby & P. Mutascio (Eds.), *Looking in, reaching out: A reflective guide for community service-learning professionals* (pp. 231–253). Providence, RI: Campus Compact.

Pearce, W. B. (2001). *Reflections on the role of "dialogic communication" in transforming the world.* Unpublished manuscript, The Fielding Institute, Santa Barbara, CA.

Perry, W. (1970). *Forms of intellectual and ethical development in the college years.* New York, NY: Holt, Rinehart, and Winston.

Pigza, J. M. (2010). Developing your ability to foster student learning and development through reflection. In B. Jacoby & P. Mutascio (Eds.), *Looking in, reaching out: A reflective guide for community service-learning professionals* (pp. 73–94). Providence, RI: Campus Compact.

Preskill, S., & Brookfield, S. D. (2009). *Learning as a way of leading: Lessons from the struggle for social justice.* San Francisco, CA: Jossey-Bass.

Rice, K. (2010). Becoming a reflective community service-learning professional. In B. Jacoby & P. Mutascio (Eds.), *Looking in, reaching out: A reflective guide for community service-learning professionals* (pp. 1–16). Providence, RI: Campus Compact.

Roberts, D. C. (2007). *Deeper learning in leadership: Helping college students find the potential within.* San Francisco, CA: Jossey-Bass.

Schoen, D. (1983). *The reflective practitioner: How professionals think in action.* London, England: Temple Smith.

Schoen, D. (1987). *Educating the reflective practitioner.* San Francisco, CA: Jossey-Bass.

Tierney, W. G., & Rhoads, R. A. (1993). Postmodern and critical theory in higher education: Implications for research and practice. In J. C. Smart (Ed.), *Higher education: Handbook of theory and research* (pp. 308–343). New York, NY: Agathon.

Vogelgesang, L. J., & Astin, A. W. (2000). Comparing the effects of community service and service-learning. *Michigan Journal of Community Service-Learning, 7*(1), 25–34.

JULIE E. OWEN *is associate professor of leadership studies and senior scholar for civic engagement and the Center for the Advancement of Well-Being at George Mason University.*

4

This chapter provides a theoretical orientation and practical advice about community partnerships by linking the literature of community engagement with that of leadership. The author introduces the POWERful model for community engagement.

Community Partnerships: POWERful Possibilities for Students and Communities

Jennifer M. Pigza

The theory and practice of service-learning have grown in breadth and depth since this pedagogy first entered American higher education in the 1970s. Included in this development is the evolution of how service-learning professionals think about the nonprofits, governmental agencies, international nongovernmental organizations (NGOs), schools, and neighborhoods where service-learning occurs. Jacoby (2003) asserts that service-learning initiatives "must be grounded in a network, or web, of authentic, democratic reciprocal partnerships" (p. 6). Faculty and staff in secondary and higher education do not merely identify *placements* for our students to do good work, but establish *partnerships* that transcend a particular student, group, course, or academic term. As educators discern whether service-learning is a fitting pedagogy to a particular course or program's leadership learning outcomes, they are wise to consider the role and process of community partnerships.

This chapter provides a theoretical orientation and practical advice about community partnerships by linking the literature of community engagement with that of leadership. Not only will this assist readers in deepening their knowledge of community partnerships for service-learning, but this linkage suggests a fundamental orientation: *Community partnerships for community engagement are the most generative when they are grounded in the models of 21st-century leadership.*

After answering some initial questions about community partnerships, this chapter offers two frameworks for leadership educators to consider when developing community partnerships: impact-oriented engagement and POWERful community engagement. The third section reviews

NEW DIRECTIONS FOR STUDENT LEADERSHIP, no. 150, Summer 2016 © 2016 Wiley Periodicals, Inc., A Wiley Company
Published online in Wiley Online Library (wileyonlinelibrary.com) • DOI: 10.1002/yd.20170

characteristics of effective community partnerships, which is followed by a discussion of practical considerations, resources, and partnership opportunities beyond service-learning. The conclusion returns to the premise of this chapter that partnerships can be models of leadership in action and offers reflective questions based in the social change model of leadership development (Higher Education Research Institute [HERI], 1996; Komives, Wagner & Associates, 2009).

Initial Questions About Community Partnerships

Service and service-learning typically occur in a context an organization external to the college, university or school, and as such, require forming some kind of partnership to engage students in that setting. For example, a class cannot simply show up at a nonprofit organization without prior arrangement and deeper conversations about purpose and process. Clarifying some common questions will set the context before delving into theoretical foundations of community partnerships for service-learning.

Who Are Possible Service-Learning Partners?   Community partners can be nonprofits, governmental agencies, international NGOs, schools, and neighborhoods. Community partners may be in the same city, across the county, in another state, or around the world. The choice of partner should be connected to the learning goals of the leadership course or program. In some instances, the concept of community partner may include other campus-based entities who are working for social change. For the purposes of this chapter, however, the focus will be on community partners external to the high school or college or university.

How Do I Identify Community Partners?   Your institution's office of service-learning or community engagement is an excellent starting point, as well as academic departments that have field-based curricula and a campus-community liaison office. Local chapters of United Way or social service networks may be gateways to identifying potential community partners. The effort to initiate a community partnership may be daunting to leadership educators new to service-learning, so joining an existing partnership may be advisable. Also note that many school systems or higher educational institutions may have a coordinated system of outreach so that local organizations are not overwhelmed by good intentions and so that service efforts are distributed in ways that meet community needs and goals.

What Kind of Service Can My students and I Offer an Organization? Service-learning literature generally refers to direct, indirect, and nondirect forms of service (Jacoby & Associates, 1996). Direct service engages students directly with the clients of a particular organization (doing oral histories with senior citizens). Indirect service involves students working on projects in the "back of the house" (organizing the audio library of oral histories). In nondirect service, students assist in advocacy or education related to a social issue (promoting the history project to local news outlets). The more appropriate question here is: What kind of service does my community partner want? And with that reordering of priorities from the campus to the community, the work of community partnership begins.

Impact-Oriented Engagement and Partnerships

One of the key values that defines service-learning is the notion of reciprocity, which indicates that both parties in the service relationship mutually benefit from the service-learning experience. Students benefit from knowledge and skill development, practical experience, application of theory, and personal development on a variety of dimensions. Community partners benefit from a completed project, increased service to a client population, a research project, outreach, and many more possibilities. In practice, however, students typically receive greater benefit than the people or the organizations they serve. Several scholars, including Longo and Gibson (2011), Mitchell (2008), and Stoecker, Loving, Reddy, and Bollig (2010), challenge this disproportionate reciprocity.

Mitchell (2008) believes that service-learning pedagogy should be more assertive and "unapologetic in its aim to dismantle structures of justice" (p. 50). For example, a service-learning project that provides tutoring to a school serving low-income families must not only provide high-quality service, but students must also engage in systemic questions about the nature of poverty, the school to prison pipeline, and how racism and poverty may intersect in a particular community. Community engagement scholars and practitioners are recasting service-learning, community-based research, and other forms of engaged pedagogy in the framework of impact and transformation. An impact-oriented framework finds direct service to be necessary but not sufficient in terms of maximizing the community benefit that can come from service-learning.

Stoecker and Beckman (2009) differentiate between outputs, outcomes, and impact when advocating an impact-orientated framework for community-based research. The shift is also occurring in service-learning. Table 4.1 offers three examples of how service-learning progresses from outputs (immediate products of service), to outcomes (evidence of mid-term progress), to impact (long-range community development goals).

Table 4.1 exhibits a core belief of the impact-oriented framework: While short-term outputs are necessary, if they take place outside the context of a larger impact-oriented trajectory, then their potential community benefits are unrealized. Leadership educators who are designing service-learning should consider how each particular initiative is a collaborative effort with a community partner toward its long-term goals. For example, while a canned food drive may generate needed food for a local pantry, if

Table 4.1   Differentiating Outputs, Outcomes, and Impact

Examples of Change Areas	Outputs (immediate products)	Outcomes (mid-term progress)	Impact (long-term community development goals)
Youth Education	Number of children tutored and total hours of tutoring	Increased performance on standardized tests	Development of a college-going culture
Health and Wellness	Results of a neighborhood health survey	Increase in home cooking by parents who take a healthy cooking class	Decrease in rates of obesity and obesity-related illnesses
Environmental Sustainability	Increase in recycling participation in a housing development	Installation of a bio-digester which converts compostable food waste for energy	Creating a culture of sustainability

that is consistently the only activity that you contribute to the partnership, you may not adequately be contributing toward the long-term change that your partner organization seeks.

What if the notion of impact were at the heart of how educational institutions collaborated with community organizations and municipalities? Many campuses and organizations are now turning to the collective impact framework for social change (Kania & Kramer, 2011) in which a five-element process guides a group of people and organizations to create lasting change. In the model are resonances of the social change model of leadership development (HERI, 1996) and adaptive leadership (Heifitz & Linsky, 2002).

- Common agenda—collectively identify a problem and create a vision for addressing it
- Shared measurement—track progress with an eye toward continuous improvement
- Mutually reinforcing activities—maximize efforts by coordinating efforts
- Continuous communication—building trust among the institutions and individuals
- Backbone support—a central team coordinates the group's efforts

My own campus, Saint Mary's College of California, is currently using the collective impact framework to develop place-based initiatives with community partners in three communities where we have existing collaborations and desire to establish a more robust presence and long-term commitments. Collective impact's success is marked by its strategic approach to change and step-wise progression through actions and data-driven decision-making. The challenge of such a model is that it may not be organic enough to respond to emergent opportunities and may not match the cultures of educational or community organizations.

POWERful Community Engagement as Transformative Leadership

The clearest linkage between leadership theory and community partnerships for service-learning is the development of the Transformational Evaluation Relationship Scale (TRES) (Clayton, Bringle, Senor, Huq, & Morrison, 2010) which is grounded in the concept of transformative leadership (Burns, 1978) and its application to community partnerships (Enos & Morton, 2003). The TRES framework differentiates between exploitative, transactional, and transformative partnerships.

An exploitative relationship reflects a disproportionate allocation of power and benefit to one partner (the lopsided reciprocity mentioned earlier). Transactional relationships are short-term, limited, project-based, and work within systems. Transformational relationships are long-term, dynamic, issue-based, and create new systems and group identities. In Stoecker and Beckman's (2009) language, exploitative relationships are focused on benefitting students and the institution rather than the community partner, transactional relationships are focused on outputs and outcomes, and transformational relationships are focused on impact. The differences between transactional and transformational partnerships are represented in the Table 4.2.

POWERful Community Engagement (adapted from Pigza, 2016) advocates that the entire enterprise of service-learning and other forms of community engagement are grounded in transformative partnerships. The cyclical nature of the POWERful Community Engagement image (Figure 4.1) reminds all constituents in a partnership (students, faculty, staff, and community partners) that their efforts are not linear. Echoing the experiential learning cycle (Kolb, 1981), POWERful Community Engagement thrives on an ongoing cycle of action and reflection that addresses five

Table 4.2   Transactional and Transformative Partnerships

Transactional Partnerships	Transformational Partnerships
Short-term	Long-term, indefinite
Project-based	Issue-based
Limited commitments	Dynamic open commitments
Work within systems	Create new systems
Maintain separate identities	Create group identity
Accept institutional goals	Critically examine goals

Source: Adapted from Clayton, Bringle, Senor, Huq, and Morrison (2010).

Figure 4.1.   POWERful Community Engagement

Source: Adapted from Pigza (2016).

elements: partnerships, objectives, working, evaluation, and reflection. The image also gives prominence to partnerships, because partnerships are "the starting and returning point that encircles each succeeding step" (Pigza, 2016, p. 94).

While the cyclical image of POWERful Community Engagement evokes the iterative process of this work, the bold inclusion of the word *power* draws attention to the role that power has in community engagement, including service-learning. To what degree is power acknowledged and shared in the partnership? How does the process of your relationship development and individual initiative development reflect shared power? *Power* also speaks to the possibilities of impact-oriented community engagement which has the potential to transform students, faculty, the disciplines, institutions, and communities. Attending to both of these notions of power as you embark in service-learning partnerships will create an opening for deeper student learning and more purposeful community impact.

Although this chapter is primarily concerned with community partnerships, Table 4.3 provides key questions to guide the development of POWERful Community Engagement and service-learning in leadership education. Again, without a strong partnership, the remaining elements of the engagement cycle are impossible.

These five elements of POWERful Community Engagement—partnership, objectives, working, evaluation, and reflection—are only successful when the central concerns of power are addressed throughout every

Table 4.3   POWERful Community Engagement Considerations

Partnerships	• What assumptions and expectations might program coordinators, faculty, community partners, community members, and students bring to a community engagement relationship? • In what ways can the growing relationship with a community partner reflect equal participation and ownership of the process? • How does our partner's community development goal match our abilities and interest as a faculty or staff?
Objectives	• How can all parties' goals and objectives matter? • How do you integrate your student learning goals with a community partner's impact goals? • Can service-learning, or perhaps another form of engagement, contribute to advancing a community partner's desired impact? • How do these goals need to be prioritized or sequenced? • What are reasonable short- and long-term action steps?
Working	• Have students, faculty, community partners, and community members fully agreed to an action plan and does everyone understand their responsibilities? • How can program coordinators and faculty engage community partners in facilitating and witnessing the growth and development of students? • How might your community engagement work be effective in telling the story of your students, school, or community partner?
Evaluation	• To what degree has the community engagement work contributed to the desired impact? • How is student learning evaluated and assessed? • How will you and your community partners continuously evaluate the partnership itself?
Reflection	• How have program coordinators, faculty, students, and community partners intentionally engaged in reflection throughout the process? • Does the reflection provide openings for personal, academic, and communal learning? • How does this reflection influence the continual formation of the partnership and your collective community engagement efforts?

Source: Adapted from Pigza (2016).

aspect of the partnership. Who is included in this process? To what degree are all voices and perspectives valued? How do the efforts of the partnership affect marginalized groups and individuals? What kind of (and whose) knowledge is given preference in the process? Questions of power can also be overlaid into the characteristics of effective partnerships.

Characteristics of Effective Partnerships

Clayton et al. (2010) proposed nine dimensions of transformative partnerships and a rubric for ongoing reflection and assessment. These nine dimensions include both individual and group level considerations such as developing a common agenda and outcomes, work and identity formation, managing conflict, and satisfaction with personal and organizational change. Loyola University New Orleans developed a partnership rubric that focuses on relationships, capacity, outcomes, and assessment (Brotzman, Deegan, & Mack, 2015). Jones (2003) identified principles of exemplary partnerships, which include time, fit, attention to power dynamics, communication, acknowledging expertise, and evaluation and assessment.

Asset-Based.   Rather than a charity-oriented model (Morton, 1995) that conceives of the community as broken and higher education as an expert fixer, an asset-based model draws on empowerment, antioppressive principles, and citizen-driven approaches (Donaldson & Daugherty, 2011). An asset-based approach relies on the local wisdom and knowledge of communities to name their vision and goals, to identify their strengths and opportunities, and to collaborate to develop and execute a plan of action. Service-learning is not about the knowing academy helping the unknowing public, but rather it is about two types of knowing joining forces toward community change. For example, and asset-based approach to a community partnership conversation would ask questions such as: What are you most proud of at your organization? How might a service-learning project contribute to your existing goals and programs? Can one of your staff provide an introduction to the neighborhood to our students?

Reciprocal.   As stated previously, the concept of reciprocity (Jacoby & Associates, 1996) asserts that in service-learning both the student and the community partner benefit as a result of the service. A community partnership that is reciprocal also reflects Rost's (1991) notion that leadership is not hierarchical and directive but rather that the exercise of leadership is process-oriented and grounded in collaboration and relationships that can be influential across the network. When considering reciprocity, consider the balance of benefits at the individual level, group level, and community level. Honest conversations with all parties to the service-learning initiative, in addition to more formal methods of assessment are ways to determine the extent of mutual benefit both at a point in time (this semester) and over time (after a multiyear project).

Focused and Sustainable.   POWERful community engagement avoids one-time contributions to community partners and does not shift from one partner to another each semester. Rather, it focuses on long-term relationships and actions that contribute to community impact goals. Often, faculty and staff choose to join an existing partnership so that their contributions are part of a network of activity. One way to think about how a partnership is sustainable is to reflect upon how working with a community partner over time represents an adaptive leadership approach. For example, perhaps a leadership course is taught each semester, but that the instructors rotate. An approach to sustainability would to make a long-term commitment to a community partnership that would remain in place regardless of the instructor.

NEW DIRECTIONS FOR STUDENT LEADERSHIP • DOI: 10.1002/yd

Free of Media Exploitation.   Quite often what communities need to build long-term capacity are projects that do not create exciting short-term news. Images of a "fill the courtyard" food drive, or of a smiling student tutoring a child, or a basketball team building a new playground are frequently used by universities and schools to promote their public service mission. As educators and their partners develop relationships, they must remain alert to the ways that a well-meaning photo opportunity becomes an exploitative experience for the individuals photographed or of the partnering organization itself. Community partners are not props, educators are their collaborators in working to attain communities' most important goals.

Practical Considerations and Resources

Leadership educators who aspire to incorporate service-learning into their courses and programs may be daunted by the notion of developing transformational community partnerships in addition to their regular duties. Here is where a collaboration with campus networks can be helpful. Consult with campus colleagues who work in service-learning and community engagement before embarking on service-learning in your leadership course or program. It may not be your individual responsibility to develop and foster a partnership.

At Saint Mary's College of California, for example, faculty and staff who are interested in initiating service-learning meet with staff of the Catholic Institute for Lasallian Social Action (CILSA, n.d.), the college's center for community engagement and social justice education. CILSA staff manage not only the basics, such as memoranda of understanding and insurance liability, but also provide pedagogical support and training to faculty and staff to design and implement high-quality community engagement. The staff are in relationship with dozens of community partners and are in deeper long-term partnerships with many. Often, a course or program (such as a leadership course with service-learning) is just one activity which contributes to larger purposes of the partnership.

In other words, one way to advance service-learning in leadership education is to place educators not as the main facilitators of a partnership, but as contributors to a larger long-term partnership. The practical reality remains that leadership educators are responsible for maintaining a relationship with the individuals with whom they work at a community agency, but this particular initiative with them would be one element within a constellation of partnership activities that all contribute to long-term community impact.

The development of impact-oriented POWERful community partnerships will also reveal additional possibilities for community engagement. Service-learning is just one aspect of community engagement. Stanford University's Haas Center for Public Service (n.d.) has identified five types of purposeful educational activities beyond direct service. They include:

activism, public-benefiting scholarship, policy/politics, philanthropy, and social entrepreneurism. A relationship with a community partner can lead to multiple types of engagement that might also contribute to your leadership learning goals.

Conclusion: The Seven Cs of Partnership

The social change model of leadership development (HERI, 1996) (see Chapter 8) is an apt leadership framework to guide the development of community partnerships for service-learning and other engagement activities. Both the social change model of leadership development and impact-oriented POWERful service-learning are founded in a desire to create positive social change through collaborative processes grounded in values. Leadership educators can draw upon their knowledge of the social change model when initiating and nurturing community partnerships. The following questions might serve as a reflective conversation with community partners and students:

- How are the individual values of consciousness of self, congruence, and commitment evident in my own actions in the partnership?
- Have we invested significantly in developing our collaboration and common purpose?
- Have we increased our capacity to have controversy with civility?
- How does our collective work increase the livelihood and well-being of citizens—those with us now and those of the future?
- How does our partnership reflect the notion of an ensemble?

Reflective questions such as these can be developed utilizing other leadership theories, as well. Engaging students in a critical conversation such as this provides a learning opportunity in which they can integrate service-learning experience with academic content. It would also invite an evaluation and assessment of their individual and collective efforts with a community partner. Here is where the possibilities of service-learning dwell. Community partnerships provide the foundation.

References

Brotzman, K., Deegan, J. & Mack, H. (2015). *Community engagement partnership rubric.* New Orleans, LA: Loyola University New Orleans.
Burns, J. M. (1978). *Leadership.* New York, NY: Harper & Row.
Catholic Institute for Lasallian Social Action. (n.d.). Catholic Institute for Lasallian Social Action. Retrieved from www.stmarys-ca.edu/cilsa
Clayton, P. H., Bringle, R. G., Senor, B., Huq, J., & Morrison, M. (2010). Differentiating and assessing relationships in service-learning and civic engagement: Exploitative, transactional, or transformational. *Michigan Journal of Community Service-Learning,* 16 (2), 5–22.

Donaldson, L. P., & Daughterty, L. (2011). Introducing asset-based models of social justice into service learning: A social work approach. *Journal of Community Practice, 19*, 80–99.

Enos, S., & Morton, K. (2003). Developing a theory and practice of campus community partnerships. In B. Jacoby & Associates (Eds.), *Building partnerships for service-learning* (pp. 20–41). San Francisco, CA: Jossey-Bass.

Haas Center for Public Service. (n.d.). *Pathways of public service.* Retrieved from https://haas.stanford.edu/about/mission-and-principles/pathways-public-service

Heifitz, R. A., & Linsky, M. (2002). *Leadership on the line: Staying alive through the dangers of leading.* Boston, MA: Harvard Business Review Press.

Higher Education Research Institute. (1996). *A social change model of leadership development (Version III).* Los Angeles, CA: University of California Los Angeles, Higher Education Research Institute.

Jacoby, B., & Associates. (1996). *Service-learning in higher education: Concepts and practices.* San Francisco, CA: Jossey-Bass.

Jacoby, B. (2003). *Building partnerships for service-learning.* San Francisco, CA: Jossey-Bass.

Jones, S. R. (2003). Principles and profiles of exemplary partnerships with community agencies. In B. Jacoby (Ed.), *Building partnerships for service-learning* (pp. 151–173). San Francisco, CA: Jossey-Bass.

Kania, J., & Kramer, M. (2011, Winter). Collective impact. *Stanford Social Innovation Review, 9*, 36–41.

Kolb, D. A. (1981). Learning styles and disciplinary differences. In A. W. Chickering & Associates (Eds.), *The modern American college: Responding to the new realities of diverse students and a changing society* (pp. 232–255). San Francisco, CA: Jossey-Bass.

Komives, S. R., Wagner, W. & Associates. (2009). *Leadership for a better world: Understanding the social change model of leadership development.* A publication of the National Clearinghouse for Leadership Programs. San Francisco, CA: Jossey-Bass.

Longo, N. V., & Gibson, C. M. (2011). *From command to community: A new approach to leadership education in colleges and universities.* Medford, MA: Tufts University Press.

Mitchell, T. D. (2008). Traditional vs. critical service-learning: Engaging the literature to differentiate two models. *Michigan Journal of Community Service-Learning, 14*(2), 50–65.

Morton, K. (1995). The irony of service: Charity, project, and social change in service-learning. *Michigan Journal of Community Service-Learning, 2*, 19–32.

Pigza, J. M. (2016). The POWER model: Five core elements for teaching community-based research. In M. Beckman & J. F. Long (Eds.), *Community-based research: Teaching for community impact* (pp. 93–107). Sterling, VA: Stylus.

Rost, J. C. (1991). *Leadership for the twenty-first century.* Westport, CT: Praeger.

Stoecker, R., & Beckman, M. (2009, February 9). *Making higher education civic engagement matter in the community* [Web log post]. Retrieved from http://www.compact.org/wp-content/uploads/2010/02/engagementproof-1.pdf

Stoecker, R., Loving, K., Reddy, M., & Bollig, N. (2010) Can community-based research guide service-learning? *Journal of Community Practice, 18*, 280–296.

JENNIFER M. PIGZA is the director of the Catholic Institute for Lasallian Social Action and a graduate faculty member in MA and EdD in leadership at Saint Mary's College of California.

NEW DIRECTIONS FOR STUDENT LEADERSHIP • DOI: 10.1002/yd

5

As service-learning has moved from the margins to the mainstream of education, programs once led by students are now coordinated by administrators, faculty, or leadership development staff. This chapter calls for the return of student-led service.

Reimagining Leadership in Service-Learning: Student Leadership of the Next Generation of Engagement

Magali Garcia-Pletsch, Nicholas V. Longo

Service-learning has moved from the margins to the mainstream in higher education, but during this growth, student leadership of campus service programs has shifted to administrators or faculty. It was not always this way. Students were at the forefront during the initial stages of the efforts to promote community service-learning across colleges and universities (Fretz & Longo, 2010). Although this shift away from students seems warranted for tactical advances in what has now been termed a civic engagement movement (Saltmarsh & Hartley, in press), for this movement to reach its civic—and, ultimately, transformational—potential, a course correction is in order.

In this chapter, we argue for service-learning to return to its democratic roots by unleashing the power of students to provide leadership in the educational process. After reviewing the origins of student leadership in service-learning, we offer examples from our work at Providence College and programs at other institutions, which are creating spaces that empower students to make longer-term commitments as leaders in community engagement through the academic curriculum. When part of a sustained, developmental approach, involving students as leaders of their own community-based learning not only supports the civic learning of students, but can also shape the next generation of engagement in higher education.

New Directions for Student Leadership, no. 150, Summer 2016 © 2016 Wiley Periodicals, Inc., A Wiley Company
Published online in Wiley Online Library (wileyonlinelibrary.com) • DOI: 10.1002/yd.20171

Rooted in Students, Increasingly Disconnected

On January 6, 1981, Wayne Meisel, then a recent college graduate, began a "Walk for Action" that took him by foot to dozens of colleges and universities throughout the Northeast. Through these visits, Meisel began to make a novel argument against the dominant narrative that young people were apathetic and self-centered. He was finding that students were not actually apathetic, but were plagued by "structural apathy"; meaning young people cared about public issues, but their institutions were not organized to provide them with opportunities to foster their idealism, most especially through community service (Hartley & Harkavy, 2011).

Soon thereafter Meisel cofounded the Campus Outreach Opportunity League (COOL) in 1984—a year before university presidents founded Campus Compact—to support student-led community service programs on campuses throughout the United States (Liu, 1996). In reflecting upon the dramatic founding of the COOL and other student-led efforts, Goodwin Liu (1996) notes, tellingly, "*students* catalyzed the contemporary service movement in higher education" (p. 6). Yet by the late 1980s, students began to lose the prominent role in the most significant service initiatives in higher education.

Liu (1996) acknowledges that faculty and administrators began taking over the leadership of the movement in the interests of consistency and sustainability. This shift was articulated in a report by Campus Compact, *Integrating Public Service with Academic Study: The Faculty Role* (Campus Compact, 1990). As the title suggests, the report argued for the importance of addressing "structural issues such as rewards and incentives for faculty involvement" in community service (Hartley & Harkavy, 2011, p. 74).

This focus on institutionalization has only deepened in the more than 25 years since, evidenced by:

- Decades of faculty research in a growing number of research journals, starting with the *Michigan Journal for Community Service-Learning* and research conferences, such as the International Association for Research on Service Learning and Community Engagement (IARSLCE)
- The growth of centers for service-learning and civic engagement to where nearly all (96%) of colleges and universities that are members of Campus Compact report having such a center (Campus Compact, 2012)
- The development of tools and awards for recognition, such as the Carnegie Community Engagement Classification, which has recognized 361 campuses as of 2015 (Carnegie Foundation for the Advancement of Teaching, 2015)

Although institutionalization is essential to sustaining an engaged campus, these kinds of changes have not had a particularly positive effect on student voice and leadership on campuses. As Liu (1996) explains:

"Institutionalization gradually shifts control and resources away from students to people who have formal power and bureaucratic authority on campus" (p. 18). He then questions "whether or not institutionalization has dampened student leadership on individual campuses" (p. 18), an observation that seems even more prescient today given the current threats to the civic mission of higher education. One might further question, what is the role of student leadership, for example in project teams, and what do students learn about leadership in the current structures?

The institutionalization of academic service-learning does not necessarily lead to a decrease in student leadership (although this is an issue in need of further study). Yet, when it comes to leadership in colleges and universities today, students are most often given passive roles as *customers* and *consumers*, even as part of engagement practices such as service-learning. Mirroring larger societal trends, colleges and universities are witnessing the rise of marketplace values as higher education is under increasing pressure to move further away from their civic missions. This is seen most tellingly in declining public financial support, and the corresponding increasing costs of higher education with the subsequent staggering amounts of student debt. Partly as a consequence of these fiscal realities, economic efficiencies and "workforce preparation" are paramount in educational decision-making, trends that further reinforce the commodification of education. A culture that values professional success—usually measured by students finding a job in a well-paying field—has steadily taken hold (Barber, 2015; Levine, 2015).

This culture has also helped fuel a rise in specialized, professional practice throughout higher education that de-emphasizes the importance of the contributions made to community and civic life. With this growth of specialized fields of knowledge, the link between learning and social purpose has become increasingly separated. Ultimately, these changes see students as consumers, rather than producers of their education.

More practical issues also challenge student leadership when it comes to making longer-term commitments to engagement: namely, the "problem of time." This recalls the story of university administrator Herman Blake attempting to set up internships for some of his college students from Santa Cruz at the Highlander Folk School, the educational center best known for its work in the civil rights movement. Blake thought a partnership with Highlander would be an ideal learning experience for his students, but the director of Highlander at the time, Myles Horton, responded by demanding "that they stay with us for two years" (Wallace, 2000, p. 133). While making this kind of multiyear commitment is a challenge in the current structures of higher education, addressing the spirit of this request is essential to putting students at the center of civic engagement. Developing structures that enable students to immerse themselves in the community cultivates the student leadership capacity that will allow campuses to contribute to the democratic renewal of society.

NEW DIRECTIONS FOR STUDENT LEADERSHIP • DOI: 10.1002/yd

Civic Practices and Longer-Term Commitments

It is with the aforementioned history and challenges in mind, that we see the need to develop a set of civic practices for student leadership that enable longer-term commitments—putting these principles at the center of what we hope will be the next generation of engagement. This effort underscores the essential connection between leadership education and civic engagement. Too often efforts to increase "youth civic engagement" and "youth leadership" have been mutually exclusive, reflecting what has been a tendency to decouple the two concepts in theory and in practice. While there are good examples of attempts to meld civic engagement and leadership development, these frequently are seen as "add-ons" or relegated to freestanding centers outside of the core university infrastructure (Longo & Gibson, 2011).

While students continue to lead on the margins, with few exceptions, mainstream academia has denied them a significant role in defining the civic engagement movement or determining how it could be implemented on campuses. But it does not need to be this way. There are promising civic practices we can draw upon to unleash the talents of students in meaningful ways. These practices help to clarify an understanding of leadership education that is focused on developing student leadership through engagement in the community. Colleges and universities, many of which already require service-learning or community-based research from students, can build upon these efforts by linking them with a deeper model of leadership education that emphasizes civic engagement as fundamental to leadership.

Our story at Providence College in many ways mirrors the broader civic engagement trends in higher education. The Feinstein Institute for Public Service was established in 1993 (Mitchell, Visconti, Keene, & Battistoni, 2011; Morton, 2012) with a $5 million grant from a local philanthropist with the initial focus on creating the first-of-its kind major and minor in public and community service studies (Morton, 2012). Initially students played a significant leadership role, including serving as equal participants, with faculty and community partners, in a summer "pilot" that developed the curriculum for the new program.

Over the next 20 years, the Feinstein Institute evolved—and institutionalized—to where distinct organizational entities supporting civic engagement are housed together. These entities are the Feinstein Institute (now with a staff of seven and supporting several hundred service-learners each semester), the Department of Public and Community Service Studies (with an elected chair and faculty lines and more than 80 majors and minors), and a more recent department in Global Studies (also with an elected chair and faculty lines and almost 100 majors).

These times of growth and institutionalization have often led to pressures that make student leadership secondary. As decision-making becomes more formal, as Liu (1996) noted, those with bureaucratic authority have more power. It has therefore become essential to counter this tendency by embedding practices in which students develop what Harry Boyte (2008) terms "civic agency," and creating spaces for students to practice this through leadership on campus and in communities. These spaces can be understood as civic practices that empower students to mentor, support, and mobilize others to tackle real-world problems in a sustained and on-going way throughout the cultural and academic life of civic engagement programs. This entails starting with recruitment efforts that utilize scholarship funds to support student leadership, offering campus-community leadership initiatives and community-based research projects, and engaging alumni in meaningful ways.

With a comprehensive and holistic approach, colleges and universities can build developmental structures that do not see students as simply one-time consumers of their education; rather, campuses can tap into students' desire to contribute to something larger. When done well—and taken as a whole—these leadership opportunities move beyond single-service/single-course student engagement experiences (the core component of merely tactical learning and engagement) and instead provide longer-term commitments to civic engagement (which is more likely to be transformational). As a result, these types of sustained, developmental approaches to civic engagement are "better able to engender new civic leaders" because they create "students who invest in community through service, scholarship, and action" (Mitchell et al., 2011, p. 115).

Recruitment and Leadership Through Scholarship Programs.   Supporting student leadership can actually begin prior to students' arrival on campus through the recruitment process with the creative use of scholarship funds. Campuses that are serious about civic engagement often develop "service scholarship programs," such as Bentley University, DePaul University, Indiana University-Purdue University Indianapolis, and the national network of Bonner schools (Zlotkowski, Longo, & Williams, 2006). These programs identify and reward students involved in their communities during high school, and then ask them to make a commitment to be part of formal civic leadership programs on campus. Not unlike athletic scholarships, programs like these offer incentives for (in this case, civic) participation in high school, and also create recognized opportunities for peer leadership on campus. These scholarships should also be targeted toward those with the most need to help overcome the inequality built into civic participation and university education. Thus, a focus on student leadership can be aligned with a commitment to access and retention of under-represented groups on campus, which then builds a leadership cadre of students of color and first generation college students.

At Providence College, the Feinstein Institute offers more than $100,000 each year in scholarships for students majoring in Public and Community Service Studies. The major then asks students to play a significant role as campus and community leaders, including through involvement in several programs described below. As part of the major in Public and Community Service Studies, students begin by taking a service-learning course, and are soon in leadership positions acting as community liaisons and mentoring younger service-learners, interning at community-based organizations, conducting semester-long community organizing projects, which ultimately leads to a year-long capstone and community engagement research project (Mitchell et al., 2011; Morton, 2012).

Community Liaisons for Community Engagement.   Students then need more opportunities to get credit, funding, and compensation for providing leadership in service-learning while they are on campus. This can involve utilizing the resources available on campus, such as using federal work-study funds in creative ways, as done at Miami Dade College. But it also involves rethinking the potential assets of students in the classroom-community configuration, with students serving as liaisons for their peers in the community, as done at Providence College and a growing number of campuses.

Miami Dade College, the largest community college in the country, uses federal work-study positions through their Institute for Civic Engagement and Democracy (iCED) to support student leadership in the community. Each year, the college allocates approximately 22 work-study positions to hire "civic ambassadors" to work approximately 17 hours a week in the iCED offices on the college's seven campuses (J. Young, personal communication, October 8, 2014). Students receive professional development and play an essential role in supporting and leading the college's myriad of civic engagement efforts. Civic ambassadors help make classroom presentations about service-learning and civic engagement, provide on-going support to faculty who use service-learning, maintain regular communication with service-learning students, organize volunteer fairs and recognition events, and lead other service projects.

Likewise, students in Public and Community Service Studies at Providence College take a year-long practicum course that asks them to serve as Community Assistants, acting as service-learning coordinators and reflection leaders with community-based organizations that partner with the Feinstein Institute for Public Service. The practicum course offers students an immersion in the work of a local nonprofit community partner, along with a cohort experience with their peers and faculty/staff mentors to reflect on their community practice. Students learn the mission and history of their partner organization, understand how it is addressing critical public problems, and even write a grant to support the organization's work in the community. Similarly, the Feinstein Institute also employs Community Liaisons (CLs) who are responsible for overseeing the growing number of service-learning students across campus. As not all CLs are Public and Community Service Studies majors, the CL program is an avenue for civically engaged students in other departments to hold a leadership role connecting the College with the community. In addition to benefitting from professional

NEW DIRECTIONS FOR STUDENT LEADERSHIP • DOI: 10.1002/yd

development opportunities within the Feinstein Institute, CLs receive a tuition scholarship for their work, and several students also use their federal work-study award to provide themselves with additional financial support.

Student Leadership in Alternative Break Courses. An area where students often play a leadership role is on alternative break trips, service projects in which students lead short-term service trips with domestic and (a growing number of) international partners. While these trips have most often taken place outside the formal curriculum, this is starting to shift—putting student leadership inside courses and academic programs.

For instance, the University of Massachusetts–Amherst has created a "professorless classroom" in which undergraduate students in the UMass Alliance for Community Transformation program (who are alumni of the course) lead grassroots organizing projects during a spring course, *Grassroots Community Organizing* (Addes & Keene, 2006). The student instructors participate in two courses to prepare to lead the course: *Critical Pedagogy* in the fall semester, and then *Leadership and Activism,* which runs simultaneously with the alternative spring-break organizing course during the spring semester.

Building upon the lessons from this model, the Global Service-Learning program at Providence College, sponsored by the Feinstein Institute and Global Studies Department, has students and faculty collaborate on courses with international service-learning trips. Student trip leaders are selected by course instructors and typically have prior experience with their corresponding course or trip. In addition to four-course credits, students are paid a modest stipend to go towards the costs of their trip.

Student leaders play a vital role in spreading awareness about the program across campus, as well as recruiting a diverse group of talented and engaged students for the program. The application process is also intentionally democratic, with trip leaders working alongside an instructor to conduct interviews and having an equal voice when it comes to participant selection. Trip leaders then support the program through pre-departure logistics, fundraising, and team building. Finally, trip leaders are the primary facilitators for group reflection sessions—before, during, and after the international experience—and often serve as cfacilitators in the development of the syllabus, facilitation of the weekly classes, and evaluation of their peers.

Collaborative, Community-Based Research. These types of teaching and engagement experiences in the community can lead to opportunities for students to conduct engaged, collaborative research with faculty and community collaborators. While some undergraduate research programs are housed separately from leadership education on campus, these opportunities build essential leadership competencies such as learning to think critically, working with diverse stakeholders, and making collaborative decisions. Capstone courses are an ideal setting for this both engaged research and applied projects. For instance, in one of the earliest models, the Haas Center for Public Service at Stanford University established the

NEW DIRECTIONS FOR STUDENT LEADERSHIP • DOI: 10.1002/yd

Public Service Scholars Program in 1994 to provide guidance to undergraduate students eager to integrate their public service commitments with their academic coursework and research interests through an honors thesis capstone. Each year 10 to 15 students are admitted to participate concurrently in their departmental honors program, and a yearlong credit-bearing seminar (*Urban Studies 198: Senior Research in Public Service*) with their peers. The seminar "challenges students to explore how their research may contribute not only to the public good but also to the development of their individual civic identities" (Mitchell et al., 2011, p. 119). The program concludes with a mini-conference, "Research With a Public Purpose," where students share their thesis research with the broader community.

Likewise, the Global Studies major at Providence College requires a senior Capstone course. The bulk of this yearlong course is structured around the development and implementation of collaborative, community-based research done in teams. Early in the fall semester, students are organized into research groups, based on their personal and academic interests, and spend the rest of the year doing individual background research on their topic, developing a community-based research agenda, and starting their project, which typically culminates in a public event. Capstone teams typically self-select one (or more) community partners to work with, finalizing their research agenda only after conversations with their partners. During the weekly capstone seminar, while refining their research skills, students are also actively giving each other feedback and working together across research groups. In this way, students are both learning from their own group members, as well as their peers working in other issue areas, continuously improving their own projects through the support of their colleagues.

This can also occur on a larger scale. Portland State University requires a capstone of each graduating student, during which faculty-led student teams conduct a community-based project. Each capstone must meet the four university-wide general education learning outcomes, which include "appreciation of human diversity and social responsibility" (Kecskes & Kerrigan, 2009, p. 12). Thus, the Senior Capstone provides students the opportunity to "become actively involved in the community and ... to create a final product that is relevant to the community," using an empowering team approach that prepares them for both professional and postgraduate work (Kecskes & Kerrigan, 2009, p. 123).

Alumni Engagement.   Finally, with the growing level of student debt, campuses need to provide more postgraduate opportunities that enable students to continue to act as civic entrepreneurs, while getting debt relief and/or money for graduate school in the process. This can be done through postgraduate public service fellowships, such as those now offered at many elite liberal arts institutions. For instance, the University of California–Berkeley awards six John Gardner Fellowships for graduating seniors to work in the government or nonprofit sector along with the

NEW DIRECTIONS FOR STUDENT LEADERSHIP • DOI: 10.1002/yd

Judith Lee Stronach Baccalaureate Prize for a graduating senior to conduct a creative project that contributes to the public good.

Aside from funding fellowships—which are necessarily more limited in scale—we need to find more ways to engage alumni as leaders. A national initiative around this idea, Citizen Alum (Citizen Alum, 2015), is trying to remake the relationship between campuses and alumni, so that alumni are seen not only as "donors" but also as "doers," vital partners in building multigenerational communities of active citizenship and learning. Thus, campuses can connect with alumni who have received external awards, such as the Fulbright or Truman Scholarships, or done postgraduate service domestically or internationally through the Peace Corps, VISTA, AmeriCorps, or elsewhere—and then utilize these experiences as an aspect of alumni engagement, as done at the University of Michigan and several other institutions throughout the country.

At Providence College, the Feinstein Institute hosts young alumni for a year of national service through Rhode Island Campus Compact's AmeriCorps VISTA program. Feinstein Institute VISTAs have been, and continue to be, engaged in conducting community-based research, developing civic engagement resources, and creating/sustaining new campus-community programs and partnerships. Upon completion of their term, VISTAs receive an "Education Award," which can be applied towards paying back federal student loans or for future education. Providence College alumni are also often engaged as guest speakers, community partners, and coinstructors in courses in the Departments of Global Studies and Public and Community Service Studies.

For the past eight years, the Feinstein Institute has also facilitated a community conversation series designed for professional service providers and community activists. Through a conversational format, this "Re-Imagining Social Change" seminar focuses broadly on the service and social change/community-oriented fields, while incorporating self-reflection of participants' activist identities. While not exclusively for former students, this seminar is another example of engaging alumni, providing a space for practitioners to re-engage in the kinds of civically focused conversations and community that they were involved with as students.

Moving Forward

When students are given serious roles in the construction of an engaged campus, as seen in the programs described above, we believe that learning is more likely to have a larger public purpose. This shift involves re-imagining students as leaders, colleagues, and producers—as opposed to passive consumers of their education. It gives students a real voice in decision-making, rather than being recipients of the decisions of others. This represents a choice about the future of student leadership in higher education. We can choose to reinforce the dominant way of knowing that tends to minimize—and too often ignore—the capacities and experiences of our students, the very people we most want to engage, or, we can take student empowerment seriously as part of the larger civic mission of higher education. When the latter happens, our goal is not simply tactical advances; rather, the future of engagement becomes about transforming students, communities, institutions, and ideas.

As seen in the practices described above, students' responsibilities can include peer and campus education, course cofacilitation, community building, organizing, engaged research, mentorship, and much more. This type of sustained, developmental approach to student leadership can be transformational for a number of reasons, including actually leading to the development of new models of leadership among faculty, staff, and community partners. Thus, leadership itself begins to shift from being about position, authority, and control of institutional resources, to being about community, contributions, and relationships that impact society. The next generation can then come full circle, creating engaged campuses that empower students to join as agents of the leadership our society so desperately needs.

References

Addes, D., & Keene, A. (2006). Grassroots community development at UMass Amherst: The professorless classroom. In E. Zlotkowski, N. Longo, & J. Williams (Eds.), *Students as colleagues: Expanding the circle of service-learning leadership* (pp. 227–240). Providence, RI: Campus Compact.

Barber, B. (2015). Illiberal education. In H. Boyte (Ed.), *Democracy's education: Public work, citizenship, and the future of colleges and universities* (pp. 199–203). Nashville, TN: Vanderbilt University Press.

Boyte, H. (2008). Against the current: Developing the civic agency of students. *Change: The Magazine of Higher Learning.* Retrieved from www.changemag.org/Archives/Back%20Issues/May-June%202008/full-against-the-current.html

Campus Compact: The Project for Public and Community Service. (1990). *Integrating public service with academic study: the faculty role: A report of Campus Compact, the Project for Public and Community Service.* Providence, RI: Brown University.

Campus Compact. (2012). *Service statistics: Highlights and trends of Campus Compact's annual membership survey.* Retrieved from http://www.compact.org/wpcontent/uploads/2013/04/Campus-Compact-2012-Statistics.pdf

Carnegie Foundation for the Advancement of Teaching. (2015). *Carnegie selects colleges and universities for 2015 community engagement classification.* Retrieved from http://www.carnegiefoundation.org/newsroom/news-releases/carnegie-selects-colleges-universities-2015-community-engagement-classification/

Citizen Alum. (2015). *Doers, not (just) donors: Re-imagining alumni as allies in education.* Retrieved from http://www.citizenalum.org

Fretz, E., & Longo, N. (2010). Students co-creating an engaged academy. In H. Fitzgerald, D. L. Zimmerman, C. Burach, & S. D. Seifer (Eds.), *Handbook of engaged scholarship: Contemporary landscapes, future directions* (pp. 313–330). East Lansing: Michigan State University Press.

Hartley, M., & Harkavy, I. (2011). The civic engagement movement and the democratization of the academy. In N. Longo & C. Gibson (Eds.), *From command* to community: A new approach to leadership education in colleges and universities (pp. 67–82). Medford, MA: Tufts University Press.

Kecskes, K., & Kerrigan, S. (2009). Capstone experiences. In B. Jacoby & Associates, Civic engagement in higher education: Concepts and practices (pp. 117–139). San Francisco, CA: Jossey-Bass.

Levine, P. (2015). Jobs, jobs, jobs: The economic impact of public work. In H. Boyte (Ed.), Democracy's education: Public work, citizenship, and the future of colleges and universities (pp. 204–210). Nashville, TN: Vanderbilt University Press.

Longo, N., & Gibson, C. (2011). From command to community: A new approach to leadership education in colleges and universities. Medford, MA: Tufts University Press.

Liu, G. (1996). Origins, evolution, and progress: Reflections on the community service movement in American higher education, 1985–1995. In R. Battistoni & K. Morton (Eds.), Community service in higher education. A decade of development. Providence, RI: Feinstein Institute for Public Service, Providence College.

Mitchell, T., Visconti, V., Keene, A., & Battistoni, R. (2011). Educating for democratic leadership at Stanford, UMass, and Providence College. In N. Longo & C. Gibson (Eds.), From command to community: A new approach to leadership education in colleges and universities (pp. 115–48). Medford, MA: Tufts University Press.

Morton, K. (2012). Process, content, and community building. In D. Butin & S. Seider (Eds.), The engaged campus: Certificates, minors, and majors as the new community engagement (pp. 89–108). New York, NY: Palgrave.

Saltmarsh, J., & Hartley, M. (in press). The inheritance of next generation engagement scholars. In M. Post, E. Ward, N. Longo, & J. Saltmarsh (Eds.), Publicly engaged scholars. Sterling, VA: Stylus.

Wallace, J. (2000). The problem of time: Enabling students to make long-term commitments to community-based learning. Michigan Journal of Community Service-Learning, 7, 133–142.

Zlotkowski, E., Longo, N., & Williams, J. (2006). Students as colleagues: Expanding the circle of service-learning leadership. Providence, RI: Campus Compact.

MAGALI GARCIA-PLETSCH is the program coordinator at the Feinstein Institute for Public Service at Providence College.

NICHOLAS V. LONGO is professor of Public and Community Service Studies, and Department Chair of Global Studies at Providence College.

NEW DIRECTIONS FOR STUDENT LEADERSHIP • DOI: 10.1002/yd

6

Although students' personal passions typically determine the issue addressed by service-learning leadership initiatives, this chapter advocates for a community-centered alternative. This in-depth exploration of a leadership development course series models a community-need driven project and explores the benefits for both community and student learning.

Decentering Self in Leadership: Putting Community at the Center in Leadership Studies

Eric Hartman

Increasingly, universities offer courses that place the student more solidly in the center of pedagogical practices. This aligns well with leadership programming and coursework, as much of it focuses on personal development, locating individual values, and moving outward from a strong sense of self to then serving and working with others. While this is valuable, it may miss something vital, which is the extent to which individuals become whole through working with causes that transcend and expand their sense of self-interest. This case study suggests that working from a community-identified concern first, rather than from personal passion, often leads to deeper and broader impact for communities and for leadership development.

This chapter profiles a course sequence in a university leadership studies program that is grounded in community-centered and justice-oriented traditions (Hartman & Kniffin, 2015). The hallmark of the community-centered course sequence profiled here is that it catalyzed leadership knowledge and practice by identifying an outside issue, the detrimental effects of the orphanage tourism industry on children, for students to focus their energies. In terms of the three types of service-learning (Jacoby & Associates, 1996), students in this course sequence were not engaged in direct service (for example, serving children at an orphanage), or indirect service (for example, writing a grant to benefit an orphanage), but rather nondirect service (in this case, education and advocacy about orphanage tourism). In a

New Directions for Student Leadership, no. 150, Summer 2016 © 2016 Wiley Periodicals, Inc., A Wiley Company
Published online in Wiley Online Library (wileyonlinelibrary.com) • DOI: 10.1002/yd.20172

typical approach to leadership education, students are exposed to leadership theories and then invited to apply the concepts to a passion or topic of their choice. The presentation to the students of a thorny global problem flipped the focus from personal passions to the development of a group passion. Key leadership theories and personal exploration were integrated into the journey as students engaged in this nondirect service-learning (Jacoby & Associates, 1996). The process of working on the community-identified issue resulted in students' personal growth, including leadership development and greater self-awareness of their passions, values, and strengths.

This chapter offers a theoretical basis for this kind of course orientation, shares the engaged learning process central to the course sequence, enumerates outcomes for the students and their tangible work products, and considers lessons learned.

The Theoretical Basis for Community-Centered Service-Learning

Service-learning scholars have long claimed that community members should be driving service-learning efforts and influencing choices throughout partnerships. In Robert Sigmon's (1979) classic formulation, service-learning is premised on reciprocal learning; it only occurs when participants on both sides of any "service" relationship benefit from the interaction. While "reciprocity" and "community-driven" are phrases frequently used in the field, their regularity does not necessarily signify broadly shared meaning or intentionality (Dostilio et al., 2012). Even in the service-learning community,

> There has been growing dissatisfaction among many people both inside and outside the service learning movement since the 1990s, particularly when it comes to the issue of whether service learning truly serves communities. In the worst cases, analysts saw poor communities exploited as free sources of student education. Others worried that the "charity" model of service learning reinforced negative stereotypes and students' perceptions of poor communities as helpless. While lip service is paid to the importance of community outcomes, there are only a handful of studies that look at community impact. ... The neglect of community impact is a result of the biased focus on serving and changing students, which creates a self-perpetuating cycle (Stoecker & Tryon, 2009, pp. 3–4).

The field of service-learning has taken seriously Stoecker and Tryon's (2009) considerable empirical evidence indicating that community organizations often experience service-learners as unhelpful and sometimes even paternalistic, biased, and a resource-drain. Exclusively student-centered or volunteer-centered approaches to service have resulted in real and tangible harms (Stoecker & Tryon). For example, international public health professionals have documented multiple instances of preprofessional volunteers and service-learners interacting directly with patients and exacerbating existing medical concerns (Evert, 2014; Virak & Nhep, 2015).

Research also indicates that high-quality, community-driven service-learning experiences are desired by community organizations and can lead to identifiable outcomes (Hartman, 2015; Reynolds, 2014; Worrall, 2007). Importantly, community-centeredness is also a best practice in community-based research (Strand, Marullo, Cutforth, Stoeker, & Donohue, 2003), asset-based community development (Kretzmann & McKnight, 1993), and many approaches to international development (Chambers, 1997). In short, evidence is strong that community-centered approaches to service-learning are required if service-learning practitioners intend to build capacity, move beyond stereotypes of recipient communities, and maximize outcomes for students and other community members.

The issue of orphanage tourism represents both the danger of service that is not community-centered and an opportunity. Although young people from many parts of the world frequently volunteer in orphanages with the best of intentions, numerous harms typically result. First, a continuous cycle of volunteers who form attachments with children and then leave is bad for children's development (Better Volunteering, Better Care Network [BVBCN], 2014). Second, in several countries, there is unmistakable evidence that the influx of funds that typically accompanies volunteers' presence has led to widespread instances of child trafficking, for the purpose of creating "orphanages" (Punaks & Feit, 2014). Third, preceding the exponential growth in international service, child protection advocates had been working for decades to deinstitutionalize children, and ensure that as many children as possible have opportunities to grow in family or foster-care networks. Family and home-based alternative care situations are better for children's development, in both low- and high-resource countries (BVBCN, 2014). A global group of more than 20 child well-being organizations, including Save the Children UK and UNICEF actively discourage international volunteering in orphanages, because of demonstrated harms to vulnerable children (BVBCN, 2014).

What this issue makes incredibly evident is that good intentions and purposeful passion are never enough. Service-learning must necessarily proceed through systematic dialogue with informed and insightful community partners—and even community development experts, who should set the intention and direction of any service initiative. The orphanage tourism challenge exists because of outsiders' uninformed assumptions regarding how they can best help.

The Leadership Studies Course Sequence and Its Outcomes

During the 2014–2015 academic year, I facilitated a unique, two-semester, honors, first-year leadership studies course sequence at the Staley School of Leadership Studies at Kansas State University. Leadership, stewardship, humanitarianism, citizenship, and purposeful passion are the subjects of the course sequence. The course started with the question of how to address the real global challenge presented by orphanage tourism. Students did not know this would be the challenge when they enrolled in the leadership course. They were given the option to identify another collective challenge, but after learning about orphanage tourism and the negative effects of good intentions on children's livelihoods around the world, the students chose to work together on this particular issue.

The course was organized so students learned about the issue, considered the values involved in leading advocacy and education on the issue, and reflected on their leadership contributions to team and public activities in the process. The syllabus identified the applied and iterative nature of this course:

> The syllabus and coursework are necessarily adaptive. That is, this course is not about mastering content or focusing on a process for you and you alone. It is developed in an effort to better understand the relationship between individual and social transformation oriented toward building a better world. Being part of a continuously adaptive course framework will prepare you well for civic and professional leadership in the years to come. And, if we implement this well, we will make a real and tangible difference in our own lives and the lives of others. (Hartman, 2014a)

Student learning outcomes (SLOs) for the first semester indicated students should develop the capacity to

- Describe their personal understanding and experience of leadership
- Employ values-based conceptions of citizenship, humanitarianism, and stewardship to assess appropriate individual and group action
- Create tangible programs, policies, or initiatives designed to address wicked social or environmental issues
- Design, organize, and plan the second semester of this course trajectory (Hartman, 2014a)

Eighteen students engaged this project as part of the course during the fall term, and 16 members of that group remained with the course sequence and project through the spring. I offer here examples of how the SLOs detailed above were encouraged through working to address the challenge of orphanage tourism.

Early meetings of the course alternated between learning more about the specific challenge of orphanage tourism and considering concepts central to leadership and social change. Additionally, settling into the commitment of a large, collaborative team effort on this issue was accomplished through steady awareness-raising within the class, combined with regular check-ins and assignments. For example, students were directed to read two websites, "Children Are Not Tourist Attractions" (http://www .thinkchildsafe.org/thinkbeforevisiting/) and "Rethinking Volunteer Travel" (http://learningservice.info/videos/) and to respond to a prompt: What are you currently feeling about the prospect of the orphanage tourism awareness-raising project? Do you think the kinds of links shared above will be effective in raising awareness? What else would you like to see, or what would you like to see more of? What ideas have you had that you would like to further pursue? Is there something else that you would like to pursue with a group of four or five?

Representative student responses included:

- Given that most voluntourism is done by groups of kids our age, I believe this is the perfect project that has global impact that can be relevant right here at home. With more research I believe we can understand and tackle this issue effectively ...
- I had never heard of orphanage tourism before we started this project ... I think that as a class we can do a lot of good work together, especially in raising awareness and providing ethical alternatives ...

Class discussions and reflection assignments provoked students' thinking about the particular type of service-learning embedded in this course: project-based social change advocacy and education, rather than direct service. This was one assignment:

> Drawing on Chapters 1 & 2 from the Komives, Wagner & Associates (2009) text, as well as the class discussion on forms of service, reflect upon where you see yourself contributing in terms of charity, projects, or social change. Indicate first a way in which you have contributed and are comfortable, then share a way in which you would like to see yourself grow in capacity to contribute.

The assignment above is indicative of the exploratory assignments that were employed during the first part of the semester. These types of assignments start conversation, seed commitment, and stir ideas for stepping forward. As students responded, they were particularly struck by the imagery in a campaign by Think Child Safe. The campaign, "Children Are Not Tourist Attractions," features an image of children in a glass box, on a pedestal, surrounded by tourists taking photos of them. The students began to form ideas regarding how they would cooperate to develop an on-campus campaign, through which they would raise awareness by appearing in a glass box on campus, then hand out information and talk with passers-by about orphanage tourism.

At my urging, students organized into teams of four or five to focus on particular areas: local awareness through events, broad awareness, research, and longevity. The language of teams rather than of groups emphasized our role as a large preprofessional team charged with enacting leadership and producing tangible deliverables in response to a global challenge identified by our community partner, a broad interagency network of child protection organizations. These teams were responsible for, respectively, growing local understanding of the issue, extending that understanding beyond our campus, gaining deeper understanding of the issue for the team as a whole, and finding ways for preserving the initiative beyond our course timeline.

Several unique opportunities emerged because the students were cooperating on a nondirect service project with global implications. First, values were explored in a global context, as well as students' positions in relation to expressions of those values such as child rights. We did this in large part through consideration of human rights as expressed by Kwame Anthony Appiah (2006) in his *New York Times Magazine* article, "The Case for Contamination." Second, students were able to apply leadership best practices through their team initiatives. Writing assignments in which students responded to their peer's writing provoked student reflection on leadership and teamwork. For example:

- How can our team create a "values-based umbrella" to lay the groundwork for transformative leadership in this area (ethical global engagement/orphanage tourism)?
- How can we integrate a time limit into our vision to establish a sense of urgency?
- What can we do to keep everyone motivated and excited throughout the process, particularly in respect to working across strengths and engaging both short-term and long-term thinkers/planners? Is there a way to develop a series of short-term wins?

Third, as the fall semester came to a close, students' synthesis of readings and the experience of working on the orphanage tourism issue continued to cultivate student ownership and deeper learning. For instance, students engaged Marshall Ganz's (2007) community organizing process in mid-November. Their efforts to tell their stories of self, us, now, prepared them to translate their work on orphanage tourism to their home communities. Additionally, end of semester grades included students' ratings of one another, employing an online survey form to conduct a 360-degree analysis for each individual student's team performance.

Fourth, and related, students were asked to provide multiple and extensive forms of feedback regarding their aspirations for the spring term. Together, we codeveloped a syllabus that continued to emphasize community-driven deliverables and heightened our attention to leadership in cooperative teams.

Advancing Leadership: Orphanage Tourism and Ethical Global Service

Organizing and delivering a course sequence centered on a particular social issue not only raises the possibility that students will advance leadership on the issue; it also requires the instructor to accumulate and organize relevant knowledge. Consistent with the scholarship of engagement (Boyer, 1996), this can be accomplished in a manner that systematically mobilizes knowledge. That was the case with this course sequence. For the students and me to become educated about the relevant issues, we participated in several webinars with leaders from nonprofits focused on this issue. Links and pertinent information were then summarized in one blog post: "Why UNICEF and Save the Children Are against Your Short-Term Service with Orphans" (Hartman, 2014b).

The students collaborated on campus-based awareness-raising events, including creating a simulated glass box and sitting in it at high-traffic locations on campus, an homage to "Children are not tourist attractions" (http://www.thinkchildsafe.org/thinkbeforevisiting/). In three days, the students spoke with and distributed literature to hundreds, if not a thousand students. Students also strengthened media presence via a video, website, Twitter feed, Facebook page, an interview with a university radio program, and letters to the editor to their hometown newspapers. Six students presented at the 2015 National Impact Conference on advocacy and education.

Finally, the students' work was featured in the newsletter of the global nongovernmental organization Next Generation Nepal ("The Paradox," 2015). While this organization was not the main community partner for this nondirect service-learning project, its country director was generous in training our students and this connection proved valuable as the project moved forward.

Considering Community-Driven Service-Learning in Leadership Education

During the final course meetings, students reflected on the outcomes of their advocacy efforts and the leadership journey of the semester. One of the students offered, "If you would have said this was required of us when we started the class, we all would have dropped it right away." And yet through engaging a thorny social issue from the outset, organizing in teams small enough to ensure contributions from each member and large enough to allow creative contributions that were more than the sum of their parts, these students slowly, systematically advanced leadership—as first year students—on a challenging global issue. Their learning advanced their understanding of leadership, of themselves as leaders, and of their capacity to critically consider and engage in global efforts.

During the second semester, the students studied and reflected upon leadership insights featured in the *Harvard Business Review* and *Stanford Social Innovation Review*. This exposed students to highly relevant publications, and also continually immersed them in the challenge I offered at the beginning: "You are all honors students; you were leaders in your high schools, so doing something good, even great, is uninteresting. I want you to develop leadership capacities so that your team contributions clearly move beyond the individual capacities of your smartest or most capable team member. Together, you have the capacity to accomplish something truly excellent." One student shared her evolving insights about the value of group work:

> In the past, I've always been the one to do all the work, and putting all the work onto one person makes the whole group's grade suffer. I resented teachers for not recognizing that the more responsible students end up pulling the whole group. ... I believed that I alone could control responsibility. I did this until this leadership class, where that reign was taken by others, and the responsibility was shared. It occurred to me recently during a group session with the video team. ... I was extremely burned out on ideas ... in the past, if I didn't have any ideas, that meant the group suffered because I always took that burden myself. But another member ... saved the day. ... It showed me that others felt responsible for our group. I was astonished and relieved ... made me realize that this project wasn't just my burden: it was theirs as well. And they were prepared to take hold of it as well ... the project became a working piece that we could all be proud of. ... Since, I have been involved in other groups in other classes, and have tried to either take active parts in them or get the others in the groups involved. If they can take responsibility, the whole group will be better for it.

Student self-reports and course evaluations indicate this course model was powerful pedagogically. Not only did the course design draw from service-learning best practices, it deeply emphasized a community-centered approach by choosing a focus issue that was presented by an international coalition of child-serving organizations. To avoid reproducing stereotypes, engaging projects not desired by the community, or even producing harms in the community, university faculty and staff who employ service-learning have a profound ethical responsibility to ensure their practices are fully embraced by community members and/or community partner organizations.

Strategies for systematically engaging community voice and cooperative development in partnerships, such as fair-trade learning (FTL) standards, are available (Hartman, Morris Paris, & Blache-Cohen, 2014). Fair-trade learning refers to a set of ethical standards for community-engaged international education. It is important to note, while the FTL standards emerged through international partnerships, the process and commitments are highly relevant to domestic programming as well. There are numerous opportunities to advance transdisciplinary, cross-cultural, community-driven engagement domestically. One example is the ongoing project between Welcoming Rhode Island and Providence College, through which university students support Welcoming Rhode Island's efforts to collect and share the stories of new community members in that state (DePlante, 2013).

Community-Centered Leadership Development: Progress Not Perfection

Although this and other courses appear strong in their fulfillment of student growth and community outcomes, some skepticism is warranted. In closing this section, I offer a critique about leadership education assessment and a commentary about student-centered pedagogy.

First, the critique: More systematic longitudinal studies in leadership education, service-learning, and civic engagement would help educators know more fully what learning experiences yield the best results. When courses are systematically different from the norm at large and/or research institutions, it is not surprising to get strong student self-reports on growth and positive personal development in areas such as leadership, civic, and intercultural capacities (Kuh, 2008). When students are exposed to unconventional courses—smaller in size, centered on the students as cocontributors, and with faculty who are personally passionate about the course—students will note that something different has happened. But, how do we know what characteristics of the learning experience matter?

For example, in the earlier iteration of this leadership course, the course trajectory started with values development, leadership, citizenship, stewardship, and humanitarianism, and then moved to create space for students to develop personal passion projects. This new version of the course trajectory centered the students on a shared issue (orphanage tourism) and then explored the content of the course while students enacted leadership in teams. Is it a problem that students did not have time to explore and articulate sense of personal passions before choosing a project? Without significant longitudinal, comparative consideration of the two course models it is hard to say.

And finally, a commentary: My bias remains toward community-centered service-learning for many of the reasons stated throughout this chapter. Another compelling reason is related to who our students are. Only 40% of the U.S. population has graduated from college (Mason, 2014) with an associate's degree or higher, therefore despite campus efforts at diversification, college students remain an elite group of people. When students identify their passions without the urging to move out of their worldviews and into community-driven spaces, the projects they choose will represent a partially informed perspective, an unrepresentative slice of the country, and a tiny portion of the world.

New Directions for Student Leadership • DOI: 10.1002/yd

My concern is that it is possible to reinforce a potentially selfish, inward focus when students are asked to start with what they want to contribute to communities, rather than what communities may want or need. Personal passion is not enough to advance democracy and human rights in communities and countries. As has been argued elsewhere (Barber, 1992; Bringle, Clayton, & Bringle, 2015; Hartman, 2013), democratic citizenship and human rights are predicated upon other-affiliation (connection with unknown others) and an assumption of moral equality (our agreement to recognize and support the dignity of all comembers in our community, country, or world). As we consider service-learning, social change, and civic leadership, we must be particularly attentive to our embeddedness in community memberships and social structures. It is only through systematic dialogue with conventionally marginalized populations that we can advance civic leadership for all. A community-centered service-learning practice is progress, not perfection, toward that end.

References

Appiah, K. A. (2006, January 1). The case for contamination. *The New York Times.* Retrieved from http://www.nytimes.com/2006/01/01/magazine/01cosmopolitan .html?pagewanted=all&_r=0

Barber, B. (1992). *An aristocracy of everyone: The politics of education and the future of America.* New York, NY: Random House.

Better Volunteering, Better Care Network. (2014). *Transforming institutional care.* Retrieved from http://www.bettercarenetwork.org/bcn/details.asp?id=32465&themeID =1002&topicID=1017

Boyer, E. (1996). The scholarship of engagement. *Journal of Public Service and Outreach,* 1(1), 11–20.

Bringle, R. G., Clayton, P. H., & Bringle, K. (2015). Beyond democratic thinking: Cultivating democratic civic identity. *Partnerships: A Journal of Service-Learning and Community Engagement,* 6(1), 1–26.

Chambers, R. (1997). *Whose reality counts? Putting the first last.* Rugby, UK: Intermediate Technology.

DePlante, M. (2013, September 15). Welcoming Rhode Island: Fostering spirit of unity in immigrants' adopted communities. *Providence Journal.* Retrieved from http:// www.providencejournal.com/article/20130915/LIFESTYLE/309159968

Dostilio L. D., Brackmann S. M., Edwards K. E., Harrison, B., Kliewer, B. W., & Clayton, P. H. (2012). Reciprocity: Saying what we mean and meaning what we say. *Michigan Journal of Community Service-Learning,* 19(1), 17–32.

Evert, J. (2014). *How does global service-learning become a dis-service in health settings?* [Web log post]. Retrieved from http://globalsl.org/cfhi/

Ganz, M. (2007). *Telling your public story: Self, us, now.* Boston, MA: Kennedy School of Government.

Hartman, E. (2013). No values, nondemocracy: The essential partisanship of a civic engagement movement. *The Michigan Journal of Community Service-Learning* 19(2), 58–71.

Hartman, E. (2014a). *LEAD 502: Introduction to global development, partnerships and social change* [Course syllabus]. Staley School of Leadership Studies, Kansas State University, Manhattan, KS.

Hartman, E. (2014b). *Why UNICEF and Save the Children are against your short-term service with orphans* [Web log post]. Retrieved from http://globalsl.org/why-unicef-and-save-the-children-are-against-you-caring-for-orphans/

Hartman, E. (2015). The utility of your students: Community partners' critique. In V. Jagla, J. Strait, & A. Furco (Eds.), *Service-learning pedagogy: How does it measure up?* (pp. 231–256). Charlotte, NC: Information Age.

Hartman, E., & Kniffin, L. (2015). *What is the theory of change? 20 years of the Michigan Journal.* Boston, MA: International Association for Research on Service-Learning and Civic Engagement.

Hartman, E., Morris Paris, C., & Blache-Cohen, B. (2014). Fair-trade learning: Ethical standards for community-engaged international volunteer tourism. *Tourism & Hospitality Research, 14*(1–2), 108–116.

Jacoby, B., & Associates. (1996). *Service-learning in higher education: Concepts and practices.* San Francisco, CA: Jossey-Bass.

Komives, S. R., Wagner, W., & Associates. (2009). *Leadership for a better world: Understanding the social change model of leadership development.* San Francisco, CA: Jossey-Bass.

Kretzmann, J. P., & McKnight, J. L. (1993). *Building communities from the inside out: A path toward finding and mobilizing a community's assets.* Evanston, IL: The Asset-Based Community Development Institute, Northwestern University. Retrieved from: http://www.abcdinstitute.org/publications/basicmanual/

Kuh, G. D. (2008). *High-Impact educational practices: What they are, who has access to them, and why they matter.* Washington, DC: American Association of Colleges & Universities.

Mason, K. (2014, April 22). *Percentage of Americans with college degrees rises, paying for degrees tops financial challenges.* Public Broadcasting Service. Retrieved from http://www.pbs.org/newshour/rundown/percentage-americans-college-degrees-rises-paying-degrees-tops-financial-challenges/

Punaks, M., & Feit, K. (2014). The paradox of orphanage volunteering: Combatting child trafficking through ethical voluntourism. *Next Generation Nepal.* Retrieved from http://www.nextgenerationnepal.org/File/The-Paradox-of-Orphanage-Volunteering.pdf

Reynolds, N. (2014). What counts as outcomes? Community perspectives of an engineering partnership. *Michigan Journal of Community Service Learning, 20*(1), 79–90.

Sigmon, R. (1979). Service-learning: Three principles. *Synergist, 8,* 9–11.

Stoecker, R., & Tryon, E. (2009). *The unheard voices: Community organizations and service-learning.* Philadelphia, PA: Temple University Press.

Strand, K., Marullo, S., Cutforth, N., Stoecker, R., & Donohue, P. (Eds.). (2003). *Community-based research and higher education: Principles and practice.* San Francisco, CA: Jossey-Bass.

Virak, S., & Nhep, R. (2015, January 21). *Good intentions and tangible harms: One Cambodian's story.* Retrieved from http://globalsl.org/good-intentions-tangible-harms-one-cambodians-story/

Worrall, L. (2007). Asking the community: A case study of community partner perspectives. *Michigan Journal for Community Service Learning, 14*(1), pp. 5–17.

ERIC HARTMAN is an assistant professor at Kansas State University's Staley School of Leadership Studies and editor of globalsl.org.

NEW DIRECTIONS FOR STUDENT LEADERSHIP • DOI: 10.1002/yd

7

Grounded in a youth leadership and mentoring program, this chapter discusses the value of asset-based community development from the service-learning literature and the concept of generativity from the leadership development literature.

Intersecting Asset-Based Service, Strengths, and Mentoring for Socially Responsible Leadership

Lindsay Hastings

College students are frequently engaged in the community through local mentoring programs, as mentoring youth has become an increasingly popular service-learning pedagogical strategy among many higher-education institutions (Schmidt, Marks, & Derrico, 2004; Wells & Grabert, 2004). While many mentoring programs are designed to build resiliency in at-risk youth, mentoring has been identified as an effective practice in leadership development (Day, 2000; Dziczkowski, 2013).

This chapter will discuss the value of asset-based community development from the service-learning literature and the concept of generativity from the leadership development literature. It will then explore the literature on mentoring as a form of community engagement that has particular potential for leadership development. Finally, a mentoring program for youth leadership will be described to elucidate how strengths-based leadership mentoring effectively intersects all of these concepts. The chapter will conclude with a set of recommendations for facilitating leadership development for college students and K–12 students through a community-based mentoring program.

Asset-Based Community Development

The service-learning literature is increasingly calling for community engagement that aligns with the concept of asset-based community development (Donaldson & Daughtery, 2011; Hamerlinck & Plaut, 2014; Lewis,

2004). Traditionally, service initiatives have been focused on identifying the community's needs and deficits in order to organize ways to "help" the community. The assumption of this approach is that the goal of service is to provide something to people in need. In contrast, the goal of asset-based community development is to build the community's own capacity (Kretzmann & McKnight, 1993). Community assets include the strengths and talents of individual community members, the formal and informal associations that gather community members together (social capital), and institutions like schools, houses of faith, community centers, and private businesses (Kretzmann & McKnight, 1993).

Asset-based service-learning programs create strong relationships that value the local knowledge that community members have, rather than assuming all expertise comes from the college/university. This focus on building capacity in the community by partnering with community members whose knowledge, talents, and strengths have been acknowledged within the community is also better alignment with the social change goals of service-learning. It is also a better approach to teaching civic leadership than traditional notions of service as "giving to the poor."

Generativity and Leadership Development and the Connection to Mentoring

Generativity refers to "concern in establishing and guiding the next generation" (Erikson, 1950, 1963, p. 267). It is an important concept for leadership development for several reasons, outlined here. First, generativity has been found to be the highest predictor of social responsibility (Rossi, 2001). Generative students, who have a higher concern for establishing and guiding the next generation, are more likely to spend their time and money building a strong family, a strong workplace, and a strong community (Rossi, 2001).

Second, several strands of research indicate a connection between leadership development and generativity. The grounded-theory research that resulted in the leadership identity development (LID) model (Komives, Owen, Longerbeam, Mainella, & Osteen, 2005) described participants as having found opportunities to be generative in later-stages of their leadership development. The LID model describes a six-stage developmental process of coming to integrate the idea of being a leader with one's sense of self (Komives, Longerbeam, Owen, Mainella, & Osteen, 2006). The fifth stage in this model, the *generativity* stage, describes students who have integrated leadership into their sense of identity, and are now mentoring other student leaders who are only starting to connect with what being a leader will mean to them. Komives et al. (2006) noted that the participants transitioned out of stage four and emerged into stage five when they began to articulate a passion and a commitment to serving the larger purposes of whatever group or organization with which they were involved. Moreover, the participants

NEW DIRECTIONS FOR STUDENT LEADERSHIP • DOI: 10.1002/yd

demonstrated generativity when they concerned themselves with the continuity of their group or organization, acknowledged a responsibility for developing others, and began coaching and mentoring younger peers. Within stage five, participants demonstrated a deeper commitment to develop interdependence among individuals within the group or organization. Further, the participants viewed leadership as a process as well as a responsibility held by all group members. Subsequent literature on the LID model has recommended that leadership educators create opportunities for students to be generative, particularly providing experiences mentoring the leadership development of their peers (Komives, Longerbeam, Mainella, Osteen, Owen, & Wagner, 2009).

In alignment with the LID research, generativity scholars McAdams and de St. Aubin (1998) noted, "It seems intuitively right that some kinds of highly effective leaders owe their success to their generative capacities and inclinations" (p. 489). This research and others indicates that leadership development programs foster generativity, and therefore the social responsibility outcomes identified above. Students who engage in leadership development programs tend to have an increased commitment to develop the same kinds of skills in others and to serve the common good (Astin & Leland, 1991; Bennis, 1989; Cress, Astin, Zimmerman-Oster, & Burkhardt, 2001; Lipman-Blumen, 1996).

Finally, research on mentoring indicates a connection to both leadership development and generativity. The positive link between mentoring and leadership development is well established (Posner & Brodsky, 1992; Ryan, 1994; Seitz & Pepitone, 1996). Interestingly, the link between mentoring and generativity is demonstrated to exist on both sides of the mentoring relationship: *being mentored relates to leadership development and efficacy, and being a mentor adds to leadership capacity*. Youth who are mentored demonstrate significantly higher generativity than their peers (Peterson & Stewart, 1996). Likewise, college student leaders who mentor revealed a significantly higher level of generativity when compared against their peers (Barnes, 2014; Hastings, Griesen, Hoover, Creswell, & Dlugosh, in press). Considering the linkage between mentoring and generativity and, therefore, social responsibility (Barnes, 2014; Hastings et al., in press), the strengths-based leadership mentoring described here serves as an important tool for leadership educators in their pursuit to develop socially responsible leaders.

The Research Behind Youth Mentoring and Leadership Development

The concept of mentoring originated in Homer's *Odyssey* (1967) when Odysseus implored his wise and loyal friend, Mentor, to bring Telemachus (Odysseus' son) under his care and tutelage during Odysseus' voyage departure. While the field of mentoring research took a while to catch up to the

Eighth Century BCE epic Greek poem, seminal authors in the 1970s and the 1980s ranging from Chickering (1969) to Vaillant (1977) to Levinson, Darrow, Levinson, Klein, and McKee (1978) to Kram (1985) all documented and posited a positive relationship between mentorship and success. The vast array of mentoring research since the 1970s, however, has not rallied around a single definition. Common threads among myriad definitions of mentoring include the following: (a) each mentoring relationship is unique, (b) mentoring involves acquiring new knowledge in some form or fashion, (c) mentoring is a process (as opposed to an event), (d) a mentoring relationship is reciprocal (even if not symmetrical), and (e) a mentoring relationship is dynamic, constantly changing over time (Eby, Rhodes, & Allen, 2010). A study using data from the Multi-institutional Study of Leadership examined two types of mentor relationships: mentorship for personal development and mentorship for leadership empowerment (Campbell, Smith, Dugan, & Komives, 2012).

One of many reasons that mentoring is a good fit for service-learning programs is the emphasis on building trusting relationships that are sustained over time. Typically mentoring is considered a relationship in which a more experienced person and a less experienced protégé mutually benefit (Campbell & Campbell, 1997; Noe, 1991). A mentoring relationship is a shared experienced between two individuals, is both active and intentional, and is focused on the protégé's needs and strengths (Gardiner, Enomoto, & Grogan, 2000). The purpose of the relationship is to develop the protégé's ability to acquire knowledge, skills, and self-confidence in hopes of becoming a better student, employee, or organizational leader (Burke, 1984; Fagan & Walter, 1982). In the specific case of youth, the purpose of mentoring relationships is to prevent at-risk behaviors, develop individual competencies in order to promote positive adjustment, and facilitate integration and involvement in the community (Keller, 2010).

For the protégé, the outcomes of the mentoring relationship are higher credibility levels, greater confidence, greater strengths awareness, and human resource skill development (Barnett, 1990; Daresh & Playko, 1990; Reiche, 1986, as cited in Moerer, 2005). Specific to youth, Blinn-Pike's (2010) meta-analytic review identified three positive youth protégé outcomes commonly surfaced from well-validated studies: (1) attitude toward school and violence, (2) some academic outcomes (such as grades), and (3) parental relationships. For the mentor, the outcomes of the relationship include increased pride and satisfaction, sharpened competencies, and greater confidence (Bass, 1990; Newby & Corner, 1997). Mentoring benefits common to both mentor and protégé include: (a) reduced stress and anxiety, (b) improved self-esteem, (c) increased professional skills, (d) increased insight, and (e) greater awareness of alternative approaches (Dziczkowski, 2013).

Mentoring is considered an important tool for developing leaders (Day, 2000; Dzickzkowski, 2013; Scott, 1992). For example, Day (2000) cited a

1999 survey study of 350 companies involved in leadership development, which revealed mentoring programs as one of the most successful initiatives in the pursuit of leadership development. In Gallup's survey of over 10 million employees and supervisors, mentoring is considered one of 12 most influential practices in sustaining workplace excellence. In particular, the survey item "someone at work encourages my development" surfaced as a statistically significant factor in determining employee engagement (Wagner & Harter, 2006). Wagner and Harter (2006) asserted that personal interaction is necessary in order to adequately address the factor of "someone at work encourages my development." They articulated this notion: " ... ['someone at work encourages my development'] requires a higher degree of personal investment by the counselor in the education of his charge" (p. 81). Despite the many documented benefits of mentoring, how can mentors be purposeful in developing the protégé's knowledge, skills, and self-confidence in their role as tutor, sponsor, motivator, role model, and coach?

Mentoring as an Investment Relationship

One way to articulate the way that mentoring values parallel those in the service-learning field, such as reciprocal, mutually beneficial relationships that focus on building capacity, is the framing of mentoring as an *investment relationship*. William E. Hall, one of the recognized fathers of positive psychology, offered the idea of investment relationships in his 1965 unpublished manuscript, "The Great Experiment." During Hall's early research, he partnered with fellow positive psychology pioneer, Donald Clifton, to identify students who demonstrated success in positively influencing others. In their research of these students, Hall and Clifton recognized that all student respondents discussed "difference makers" in their lives. These authors concluded that strong, positive relationships with "difference makers" impact a person's ability to discover and develop individual talents (Hall, ca. 1965).

Hall (ca. 1965) defined relationship as the response one makes to the existence of another person and proffered that *investment* relationships, as compared to other types of relationships, are a purposeful effort to achieve higher self-realization of the greatest resource—the human resource. Hall described three levels of relationships: (1) exploratory (this would include early responses made to a person being met for the first time), (2) work-a-day (these are the relationships formed between those who meet together on a daily basis), and (3) investment (these are relationships that have the power to change people's lives). Investment relationships are somewhat analogous to what occurs in the banking business. An investment in another person yields dividends for the investor. Hall (ca. 1965) asserted that lasting, significant differences in human beings can only become a reality when one person invests time in another person on an individual basis.

Further, he posited that this is only possible if the investor's "human relations capital" is equal to or greater than the needs of the investee. Hall argued that concern for others, no matter how sincere, does not by itself guarantee favorable development.

Moving from "work-a-day" relationships (which perhaps could be considered forced mentoring) to investment relationships involves the mentor intentionally identifying talents in the investee, creating opportunities to develop those talents, and ultimately preparing the investee to become an investor, which creates a ripple effect. In addition, reflection upon the growth, development, and outcomes of the investment relationship are critical for the mentor (Hall, ca. 1965).

Remaining curious about the importance of difference makers and investment relationships, Hall and Clifton worked with local philanthropists to provide an opportunity for these students with "high human relations capital" to be paired in one-to-one relationships with local K–12 student leaders. Their goal was to establish several investment relationships and study the outcomes of such relationships. This became the birthplace for what is now the Nebraska Human Resources Institute (NHRI). Grounded in the ideals of positive psychology that champion investing in talent rather than treating pathologies (Seligman & Csikszentmihalyi, 2000), Hall and Clifton devised a unique strengths-based leadership mentoring program characterized by one high-performing leader purposefully developing the talents of another individual with leadership promise.

The NHRI Program: Designing a Mentoring Program That Fosters Leadership Development

The NHRI at the University of Nebraska–Lincoln is a well-established model of strengths-based leadership mentoring in preparing socially responsible leaders, with over 60 years of experience in leadership development and mentoring research (University of Nebraska-Lincoln, 2015). NHRI identifies and selects outstanding college student leaders and pairs them in one-to-one relationships with outstanding K–12 student leaders. The objective for the college students is to identify leadership talents within their mentees, develop their leadership capacities, and direct their developed leadership toward positive reinvestment in others.

Selection.   Deliberate, thorough, and strengths-based selection is one hallmark of NHRI and should be credited for NHRI's 60-plus years of success. Considering the demands of an investment relationship, it is critical for college students who are selected to take the mentoring commitment very seriously. In NHRI, University of Nebraska–Lincoln college students (called "counselors") are selected on the basis of demonstrating significant "human relations capital"—a capacity to positively influence the thoughts, feelings, and behaviors of others. This selection philosophy is the result of Hall and Clifton's early work at the NHRI which revealed a series of common talent themes related to human relations capital, such as sense of mission, empathy, and listening. Hall and Clifton built a selection assessment around the human relations capital themes, which is still used for selection purposes today.

Freshmen students who are interested in the program or who are nominated by current students in the program, faculty, staff, or alumni attend an orientation to learn more about the program, then are invited to engage in an hour-long interview to assess their human relations capital talent. Students whose interview results indicate strong human relations capital are paired in one-to-one relationships with K–12 students in Lincoln Public Schools who have also been identified as high potential leaders. At any given point in time, NHRI works with approximately 180 college student leaders and 180 K–12 student leaders.

While many youth mentoring programs identify "at-risk youth," this approach has the potential to focus the program on the needs and deficits of the youth in question, rather than on their assets, talents, and potential. In keeping with the asset-based community development approach advocated by the service-learning field, the youth in NHRI programs are considered to be contributors to the community and its capacity-building efforts. The K–12 student leaders (called "junior counselors") are also selected for the program on the basis of demonstrating high human relations capital, as evaluated by school principals, teachers, and guidance counselors. NHRI staff reach out to local school administrators and teachers to evaluate their students' leadership talents in areas such as building positive relationships, inclusiveness, diversity appreciation, encouraging improved classroom performance, and behavior in other students, and so forth. Once student leaders are identified, school administrators contact parents to inform them of their child's selection. NHRI staff then set up orientation sessions with selected students and their families to introduce them to the program and the student's counselor.

Operations.   College students ("counselors") are typically selected for the program as second semester freshmen and are paired with K–12 student leaders ("junior counselors") based on common interests. Each pair meets weekly for three years. The objective for the counselors is to identify leadership talents within their junior counselors, develop their leadership capacities, and direct their developed leadership toward positive reinvestment in others. Some of the college students will enroll in a course that runs concurrently with their mentoring role.

In accordance with Keller's (2010) observation that effective mentors create a meaningful relationship with their mentees as well as facilitate positive development, counselors are encouraged to spend the first 6 to 8 weeks purely focusing on building a friendship with their junior counselors. This "friendship phase" may involve discovering common interests and meeting family members and friends. Once counselors feel that a solid friendship (and more importantly, a trust foundation) has been established, then

Figure 7.1.   Investment Relationship Model

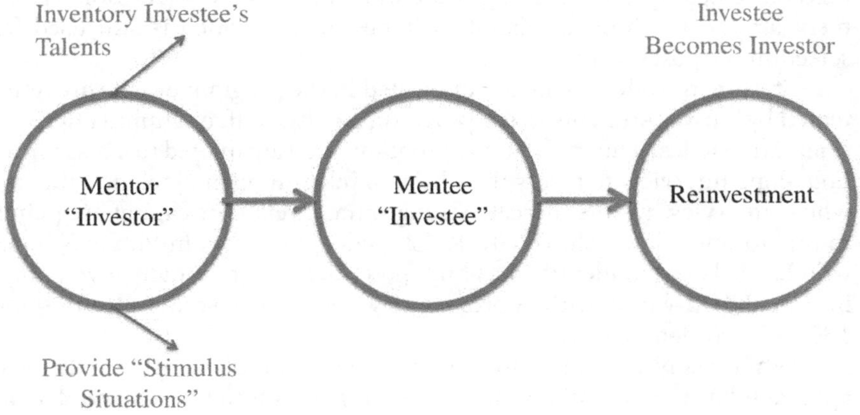

Inventory Investee's
Talents

Investee
Becomes Investor

Mentor
"Investor"

Mentee
"Investee"

Reinvestment

Provide "Stimulus
Situations"

Source: Adapted from Dodge (1986).

counselors are encouraged to more actively pursue leadership development with their junior counselors.

The counselors' first leadership development task is to identify leadership talents within their junior counselors. Counselors are encouraged to attend their junior counselors' extracurricular activities, eat lunch with them at school, and participate in family events in order to accurately observe and identify unique leadership talents. The second task is to develop the junior counselors' identified leadership capacities by creating "stimulus situations." For example, if a counselor recognizes that the junior counselor has high rapport drive, that counselor might challenge the junior counselor to evaluate the difference in response when calling others by name versus just saying "hello." Upon reflection the following week, the counselor will help the junior counselor to recognize that when rapport drive is used deliberately to call someone by name, that person ultimately feels important. The junior counselor is then encouraged to use rapport drive deliberately every day as a vehicle for helping others to feel recognized and important. The ultimate goal is for the junior counselors to become most effective at making a difference in the lives of others. The counselors invest in their junior counselors with the intention of preparing junior counselors to turn and invest in others, creating a capacity-building "ripple effect" (Hall, ca. 1965). See Figure 7.1.

Reflection. Based on the age or school of their junior counselors, counselors are grouped in "projects." For example, all college student leaders working with 10th-through 12th-grade student leaders are in *Teenage Project*. These projects meet weekly for an hour to discuss the progress of their relationships with their junior counselors. This reflection piece is designed to help each counselor study the development and outcomes of investment relationships. Weekly project meetings are also a time for counselors to receive advice and guidance regarding how to be most effective in mentoring their junior counselors. Each project also conducts monthly retreats with their junior counselors to examine positive psychology concepts. The counselors typically prepare a curriculum for the retreat (i.e., the importance of active listening in leadership), or the entire project engages in a community reinvestment project.

Training. Counselors are also given the opportunity to take a training course in interpersonal skills for leadership during one semester of their NHRI experience (commonly referred to as the "NHRI Class"). The course objectives center on self-understanding, understanding others, and investing in others. Counselors who take the course engage in scholarly discourse related to positive psychology principles such as empathy, active listening, investment relationships, strengths, and self-concept, among others. Utilizing service-learning pedagogy (Furco & Billig, 2001), course participants write each week about their reactions to course concepts and how those concepts apply in their relationships with others. Furthermore, their relationship with their junior counselor serves as the active service experience of the course. Course participants keep a weekly diary of their experiences with their junior counselors and create a final project that analyzes and evaluates the application of course concepts in their mentoring relationship.

In sum, college student leaders engage in the following four activities during their NHRI tenure in accordance with best practices in youth mentoring (Miller, 2010): (1) weekly meetings with their junior counselor, (2) weekly project meetings (college students only), (3) monthly retreats (both counselors and junior counselors), and (4) the NHRI Class.

Recommendations

Considering the predictive linkage between generativity and social responsibility (Rossi, 2001), higher education institutions would be prudent to deliberately cultivate generativity among their student populations. Community-based youth mentoring programs are perhaps one vehicle to consider. Colleges and universities that could successfully cultivate and document higher generativity among their students could make a compelling argument to business and industry for hiring their graduates. This could impact career placement success rates and ultimately help their institutions garner a competitive advantage.

While mentoring is an important tool for developing leaders (Day, 2000; Dzickzkowski, 2013; Scott, 1992), strengths-based leadership mentoring is a way to model the asset-based community development approach, preparing college student leaders to think beyond traditional notions of service to the community so they might continue to consider how to *invest* in the next generation of leaders and exercise their leadership in a generative way.

Building a successful strengths-based leadership mentoring program within not only a university community, but also its surrounding community requires deliberate thought and effort in the following four areas: (1) selection, (2) operations, (3) reflection, and (4) training. College and K–12 student selection for a strengths-based leadership mentoring program needs to involve rigorous procedures designed to assess human relations talent and positive influential promise. To prepare college students to move from mentoring to investing, day-to-day programmatic expectations need to include regular, weekly meetings between the college and K–12 students, weekly meetings among college student mentors, and bimonthly opportunities for groups of mentors and mentees to meet and for mentors to actively train their mentees in leadership development concepts. Furthermore, college students should be expected to work with the same student consistently over the course of several years in order to adequately provide an opportunity to invest in their mentees. Weekly meetings among college student mentors need to include an active reflection component, where each college student is given the opportunity to share success and frustration and to receive guidance and support from peers and program staff. Last, every incoming college mentor should receive training in interpersonal skills for leadership and investment relationship principles. These aforementioned selection, operation, reflection, and training recommendations will allow a university community to meaningfully connect with its surrounding community by mobilizing the institution's diverse resources toward building leadership capacity among community youth while at the same time preparing its own future graduates to become socially responsible leaders.

References

Astin, H. S., & Leland, C. (1991). *Women of influence, women of vision: A cross-generational study of leaders and social change.* San Francisco, CA: Jossey-Bass.

Barnes, S. R. (2014). *Exploring the socially responsible leadership capacity of college student leaders who mentor.* (Master's thesis). Retrieved from digitalcommons.unl.edu

Barnett, B. G. (1990). The mentor-intern relationship: Making the most of learning from experience. *NASSP Bulletin, 74*(526), 17–24.

Bass, B. M. (1990). *Bass and Stogdill's handbook of leadership* (3rd ed.). New York, NY: Free Press.

Bennis, W. G. (1989). *On becoming a leader.* Reading, MA: Addison-Wesley.

Blinn-Pike, L. (2010). The benefits associated with youth mentoring relationships. In T. D. Allen & L. T. Eby (Eds.), *The Blackwell handbook of mentoring: A multiple perspectives approach* (pp. 165–188). Chichester, West Sussex: Blackwell.

Burke, R. J. (1984). Mentors in organizations. *Group and Organization Studies, 9*(3), 353–372.

Campbell, T. A., & Campbell, D. E. (1997). Faculty/student mentor programs: Effects on academic performance and retention. *Research in Higher Education, 38*(6), 727–742.

Campbell, C. M., Smith, M., Dugan, J. P., & Komives, S. R. (2012). Mentors and college student leadership outcomes: The importance of position and process. *The Review of Higher Education, 35*(4), 595–625.

Chickering, A. (1969). *Education and identity.* San Francisco, CA: Jossey-Bass.

Cress, C. M., Astin, H. S., Zimmerman-Oster, K., & Burkhardt, J. C. (2001). Developmental outcomes of college students' involvement in leadership activities. *Journal of College Student Development, 42*(1), 15–27.

Daresh, J. C., & Playko, M. I. (1990). Mentoring for effective school administration. *Urban Education, 25*(1), 43–54.

Day, D. V. (2000). Leadership development: A review in context. *Leadership Quarterly, 11,* 581–613.

Dodge, G. (1986). *Priceless people: A guide for human resources development.* Lincoln, NE: Metromail.

Donaldson, L. P., & Daughtery, L. (2011). Introducing asset-based models of social justice into service learning: A social work approach. *Journal of Community Practice, 19*(1), 80–99.

Dziczkowski, J. (2013). Mentoring and leadership development. *The Educational Forum, 77,* 351–360.

Eby, L. T., Rhodes, J. E., & Allen, T. D. (2010). Definition and evolution of mentoring. In T. D. Allen & L. T. Eby (Eds.), *The Blackwell handbook of mentoring: A multiple perspectives approach* (pp. 7–20). Chichester, West Sussex: Blackwell.

Erikson, E. H. (1950, 1963). *Childhood and society.* New York, NY: Norton.

Fagan, M. M., & Walter, G. (1982). Mentoring among teachers. *Journal of Educational Research, 76,* 113–118.

Furco, A., & Billig, S. H. (Eds.) (2001). *Service-learning: The essence of the pedagogy.* Greenwich, CT: Information Age.

Gardiner, M. E., Enomot, E., & Grogan, M. (2000). *Coloring outside the lines: Mentoring women into school leadership.* Albany: State University of New York Press.

Hall, W. E. (ca. 1965). *The great experiment.* Unpublished manuscript, Nebraska Human Resources Institute, University of Nebraska–Lincoln, Lincoln, NE.

Hamerlinck, J., & Plaut, J. (2014). *Asset-based community engagement in higher education.* Minneapolis: Minnesota Campus Compact.

Hastings, L. J., Griesen, J. V., Hoover, R. E., Creswell, J. W., & Dlugosh, L. L. (In press). Generativity in college students: Comparing and explaining the impact of mentoring. *Journal of College Student Development.*

Homer (1967). *The odyssey of Homer: Translated with an introduction by Richmond Lattimore.* New York, NY: Harper & Row.

Keller, T. E. (2010). Youth mentoring: Theoretical and methodological issues. In T. D. Allen & L. T. Eby (Eds.), *The Blackwell handbook of mentoring: A multiple perspectives approach* (pp. 23–48). Chichester, West Sussex, England: Blackwell.

Komives, S. R., Longerbeam, S. D., Mainella, F. C., Osteen, L., Owen, J. E., & Wagner, W. (2009). Leadership identity development: Challenges in applying a developmental model. *Journal of Leadership Education, 8*(1), 11–47.

Komives, S. R., Longerbeam, S. D., Owen, J. E., Mainella, F. C., & Osteen, L. (2006). A leadership identity model: Applications from a grounded theory. *Journal of College Student Development, 47*(4), 401–418.

Komives, S. R., Owen, J. E., Longerbeam, S. D., Mainella, F. C., & Osteen, L. (2005). Developing a leadership identity: A grounded theory. *Journal of College Student Development, 46*(6), 593–611.

Kram, K. E. (1985). *Mentoring at work: Developmental relationships at work.* Glenview, IL: Scott, Foresman.

Kretzmann, J., & McKnight, J. (1993). *Building communities from the inside out: A path toward finding and mobilizing a community's assets*. Evanston, IL: Center for Urban Affairs and Policy Research, Northwestern University.

Levinson, D. J., Darrow, D., Levinson, M., Klein, E. B., & McKee, B. (1978). *The seasons of a man's life*. New York, NY: Knopf.

Lewis, T. L. (2004). Service learning for social change? Lessons from a liberal arts college. *Teaching Sociology, 32*, 94–108. Retrieved from http://search.proquest.com/docview /223528406?accountid=11243

Lipman-Blumen, J. (1996). *Connective leadership: Managing in a changing world*. Oxford, England: Oxford University Press.

McAdams, D. P., & de St. Aubin, E. (Eds.). (1998). *Generativity and adult development: How and why we care for the next generation*. Washington, DC: American Psychological Association.

Miller, A. (2010). Best practices for formal youth mentoring. In T. D. Allen & L. T. Eby (Eds.), *The Blackwell handbook of mentoring: A multiple perspectives approach* (pp. 307–324). Chichester, West Sussex: Blackwell.

Moerer, T. (2005). *A longitudinal qualitative study of collegiate mentoring experiences in the Nebraska Human Resources Research Foundation*. (Doctoral dissertation). Retrieved from digitalcommons.unl.edu

Newby, T. J., & Corner, J. (1997). Mentoring for increased performance: Benefits and key principles. *Performance Improvement, 36*(4), 10–13.

Noe, R. A. (1991). Mentoring relationship for employee development. In J. W. Jones, B. D. Steffey, & D. W. Bray (Eds.), *Applying psychology in business: The manager's handbook* (pp. 475–482). Lexington, MA: Lexington Press.

Peterson, B. E., & Stewart, A. J. (1996). Antecedents and contexts of generativity motivation at midlife. *Psychology and Aging, 11*(1), 21–33.

Posner, B., & Brodsky, B. (1992). A leadership development instrument for college students. *Journal of College Student Development, 33*(3), 231–237.

Rossi, A. S. (2001). Domains and dimensions of social responsibility: A sociodemographic profile. In A. S. Rossi (Ed.), *Caring and doing for others: Social responsibility in the domains of family, work, and community* (pp. 97–134). Chicago, IL: University of Chicago Press.

Ryan, L., & League for Innovation in the Community (1994). *The case for national student leadership on community college issues*. Leadership Abstracts.

Schmidt, M. E., Marks, J. L., & Derrico, L. (2004). What a difference mentoring makes: Service-learning and engagement for college students. *Mentoring and Tutoring, 12*(2), 205–217.

Scott, M. E. (1992). Designing effective mentoring programs: Historical perspectives and current issues. *Journal of Humanistic Education and Development, 30*(4), 167–177.

Seitz, S., & Pepitone, S. (1996). Servant leadership: A model for developing college students. *Metropolitan Universities: An International Forum, 6*(4), 113–122.

Seligman, M. E. P., & Csikszentmihalyi, M. (2000). Positive psychology: An introduction. *American Psychologist, 55*(1), 5–14.

University of Nebraska–Lincoln. (2015). Nebraska Human Resources Institute. Retrieved at http://nhri.unl.edu/

Vaillant, G. (1977). *Adaptation to life*. Boston, MA: Little, Brown.

Wagner, R., & Harter, J. K. (2006). *12: The elements of great managing*. New York, NY: Gallup Press.

Wells, C. V., & Grabert, C. (2004). Service-learning and mentoring: Effective pedagogical strategies. *College Student Journal, 38*, 573–578.

LINDSAY HASTINGS *is the Clifton Professor in Mentoring Research and Director of the Nebraska Human Resources Institute at the University of Nebraska.*

8

This chapter presents the Hugh O'Brian Youth Leadership (HOBY) program as a case study, examining their gradual process of shifting all programs to integrate leadership development and service. As an organization with over 4,000 volunteers and a nationwide scope, the change process was a challenge but resulted in benefits that fit the organizations' values. The social change model for leadership development (Higher Education Research Institute, 1996) was used as a guiding framework.

Hugh O'Brian Youth Leadership: Using a Theoretical Model at the Intersection of Youth Leadership Education and Service-Learning

Vicki Ferrence Ray

Although leadership development scholarship has emphasized the importance of grounding leadership programs in theoretical models, many programs have not yet made that shift. This chapter will offer the Hugh O'Brian Youth Leadership (HOBY) programs for high school students as a demonstration of how the integration of service learning informed the need for and selection of the social change model (SCM) of leadership development (Higher Education Research Institute [HERI], 1996), to both guide program design and offer as learning content to students. Both a description of the theory-based program design and the path we experienced in shifting to a theory-based program are provided. HOBY believes leadership is action, not title or position, and that no matter the leader's age, role, or sector, effective positive leadership is ultimately service to humanity for the betterment of the world. Both service-learning and the SCM have therefore been an excellent fit. The Role of Theoretical Models in Leadership Development Program Design.

When leadership development programs for youth and college students were first emerging, most were based on the skills-development approaches that were pervasive at the time (Rost, 1993). As the scholarship

NEW DIRECTIONS FOR STUDENT LEADERSHIP, no. 150, Summer 2016 © 2016 Wiley Periodicals, Inc., A Wiley Company
Published online in Wiley Online Library (wileyonlinelibrary.com) • DOI: 10.1002/yd.20174

around effective leadership has expanded, leadership development is now generally understood to be more than simply the acquisition of skills but related to one's way of being in the world and issues of human development, including intrapersonal development, interpersonal development, cognitive complexity, moral/ethical development, and identity development (Day & Lance, 2004; Halpern, 2004; Kegan & Lahey, 2009; Wagner, 2011). With this new appreciation for the complexity of leadership development as a transformational learning process rather than simply acquiring new knowledge and skills, leadership educators acknowledged that programs need to have theoretical grounding (Dugan & Owen, 2007; Posner, 2004). Evidence supporting the connection between theoretical grounding and student learning also emerged (Eich, 2008; Owen, 2008). In *The Handbook for Student Leadership Development Programs*, Dugan and Komives (2011) were unequivocal, "No longer viable are approaches to leadership education predicated on loosely defined conceptualizations, solely skill-based content, or intuitive designs" (p. 36). Leadership development scholars have suggested that the role these theoretical models play in student learning is connected to students' meaning-making, "Theory provides the overarching sense-making frame for experience. Without a theoretical framework to connect and integrate experiences there is no sense-making, and thus there can be no learning" (Day, Harrison, & Halpin, 2009, p. 7). This lends additional support to the notion that leadership theory should not only guide the design of programs, but should be taught as content to students in those programs. When students have a meaning-making structure to help make sense of their leadership experiences (including service-learning), their ability to be reflective about their experiences sets the foundation for a lifetime of learning and leadership growth (Komives & Dugan, 2014).

Although the empirical literature is clearly supportive of the benefit of theoretically grounded leadership programs, current practice does not seem to be in alignment with those findings. A 2012 study of student leadership development program design and delivery found, "Most leadership programs claim to be grounded in postindustrial relational, complex theoretical approaches to leadership, yet many (64%, $n = 57$) frequently rely on personality inventories, heuristics, and other nontheoretical (and nonleadership) approaches in program applications" (Owen, 2012, p. 11).

Introduction to HOBY

For almost six decades, HOBY has inspired young people to make a difference and become catalysts for positive change in their home, school, workplace, and community. As America's premier youth leadership development organization, HOBY has a long and impressive history of successfully motivating youth and volunteers to outstanding leadership. HOBY is an apolitical, nonreligious, all-inclusive, 501(c)(3) nonprofit organization founded in 1958 by the actor Hugh O'Brian (Walke, 2010).

NEW DIRECTIONS FOR STUDENT LEADERSHIP • DOI: 10.1002/yd

HOBY programs are conducted annually throughout the United States, and in many countries around the world, serving local and international high school students with unique leadership training, service-learning, and motivation-building experiences which vary in length from 1 to 8 days depending on the specific program offering (What Is HOBY?, 2015). HOBY also provides adults with opportunities to make a significant impact on the lives of youth by volunteering. Over 4,000 committed HOBY volunteers plan and execute the programs each year, serving both at the state HOBY affiliate level and internationally on HOBY's Board of Trustees (What Is HOBY?, 2015). Due to the selfless efforts of volunteers and the contributions of generous donors, more than 10,000 students participate in HOBY programs annually. HOBY has only 13 full-time equivalent paid staff (What Is HOBY?, 2015).

HOBY programs provide youth with unique leadership training to make a better world and a better society. Each program strives to follow the HOBY motto of teaching young leaders creatively, critically, and compassionately, "how to think, not what to think"(What Is HOBY?, 2015). Today HOBY has five program lines, described in Table 8.1.

HOBY challenges all program alumni to complete a minimum of 100 hours of community service through the Leadership for Service (L4S) Program (Leadership for Service [L4S] Challenge, 2015). Students have one year from their HOBY program attendance to perform and log volunteer hours on HOBY's L4S website. At the completion of the challenge, students receive a certificate of recognition from HOBY, the President's Volunteer Service Award, scholarship opportunities, and more. HOBY Alumni have logged over 3.5 million hours of service.

The Story of HOBY's Founding: Leadership as Service

The intersection of leadership and service at HOBY is connected to its very origins. The story of HOBY's founding remains central to its mission and operation today. HOBY alumni and volunteers know the story well; it is retold here for the reader's benefit in understanding the subsequent sections of this chapter.

In the summer of 1958, actor Hugh O'Brian received the invitation that would change his life. O'Brian, then 33, was in Winnipeg, Manitoba, parlaying his fame as television's legendary Wyatt Earp into extra income by guest-starring in a rodeo. Then the cable arrived from French Equatorial Africa: renowned humanitarian and 1952 Nobel Peace Prize winner Dr. Albert Schweitzer would welcome him at any time (Walke, 2010).

O'Brian had long admired the German doctor-missionary-theologian-musician. "I'd read so much about him," he reflects. "He was a great humanitarian who could have done anything he wanted in the world, and there he was in the middle of Africa taking care of people" (Walke, 2010, p. 13). Within 2 weeks he was on his way, by commercial airliner, bush plane, and

NEW DIRECTIONS FOR STUDENT LEADERSHIP • DOI: 10.1002/yd

Table 8.1   Hugh O'Brian Youth Leadership (HOBY) Programs

Mission: To inspire and develop our global community of youth and volunteers to a life dedicated to leadership, service, and innovation.
Vision: To motivate and empower individuals to make a positive difference within our global society, through understanding and action, based on effective and compassionate leadership.
Core Values: Volunteerism, Integrity, Excellence, Diversity, Community Partnership

The Community Leadership Workshop (CLeW)	An introductory one-day leadership program for high school freshmen, which focuses on leadership as a discipline to be explored and learned. CLeW students interact with local community leaders, participate in group learning activities, and conduct community service projects. CLeWs are organized, developed, and implemented by local business leaders, civic groups, volunteers, and HOBY alumni.
The State Leadership Seminar	HOBY's flagship program. Three 4-day seminars, for select high school sophomores, offered at the state level. Students participate in hands-on leadership activities, meet leaders in their state, and explore their own personal leadership skills while learning how to lead others and make a positive impact in their community.
Advanced Leadership Academy (ALA)	A five-day practical and experiential program open to all high school juniors and seniors. The curriculum explores how students can use their specific individual abilities to organize and lead a service or social entrepreneurship project to create meaningful change. ALA participants leave the program with a practical action project to implement on their return home, with ongoing mentoring provided to coach them through project implementation. College credit for the experience is available through George Mason University.
World Leadership Congress (WLC)	This week-long international program for rising high school seniors has been offered since 1968. Each year more than 425 students representing up to 20 countries attend the program, comprised of keynote presentations, speakers' panels, interactive workshops, field trips, and community service projects.
International Tour Program	High school and college students from across the country experience an eight-day tour to some of the world's most exciting and historic destinations. This program includes professional guided tours, practical travel lessons, international service experience, and foreign language introduction.

canoe, to the famed hospital that Schweitzer had founded in 1913 on the banks of the Ogooue River in Lambarene. The actor spent nine days at the clinic complex where Schweitzer and volunteer doctors and nurses, working without electricity or running water, cared for patients, including many with leprosy.

The doctor was impressed that the young American had taken the trouble to visit him. During the day O'Brian helped in the clinic, and in the evenings Schweitzer shared stories and life lessons with O'Brian. Schweitzer,

NEW DIRECTIONS FOR STUDENT LEADERSHIP • DOI: 10.1002/yd

then 83, who had received the 1952 Nobel Peace Prize, was concerned about global peace prospects and was convinced that the United States should take a leadership role in achieving peace. He impressed upon the young O'Brian the urgency for change and how education must teach young people to think for themselves (Walke, 2010).

It was an unforgettable nine days. And, as O'Brian departed, Schweitzer took his hand, looked deeply into his eyes, and asked, "Hugh, what are you going to do with this?" (Walke, 2010, p. 13). Two weeks after returning from his 1958 meeting with Schweitzer, O'Brian put together a prototype seminar for young leaders—HOBY. And the rest is living history.

HOBY's guiding philosophy that "the most important thing in education is for young people to learn how to think for themselves" and "not teaching what to think, but how to think" (What Is HOBY? 2015) were developed directly from O'Brian's meeting with Schweitzer. Youth leadership education to achieve long-term social change is clearly the primary goal of HOBY, but even from the very beginning there was the notion of service as an essential component of leadership. Schweitzer's work and his life reflected both leadership and service, which O'Brian recognized and emulates became embodied in his creation of HOBY.

HOBY's Continued Commitment to Service

In April 1997, then General Colin Powell led an unprecedented gathering in Philadelphia called the President's Summit for America's Future. It was at this summit that America's Promise—The Alliance for Youth was created (Walke, 2010). HOBY's commitment to America's Promise was to implement a service component at its Leadership Seminars, and ask each student to undertake a minimum of 100 hours of volunteer service within one year following their seminar. Students who complete and log their service hours on HOBY's website (www.hoby.org) receive the President's Volunteer Service Award. HOBY designated the term "Leadership for Service" with the acronym L4S to represent the organization's commitment and its associated program components.

During this time, there was an understanding at HOBY that service is a way for teenagers to apply their newfound leadership skills, and that leadership is ultimately service to humanity. Unfortunately, teenagers are often regarded by adults as not old or experienced enough to hold meaningful official leadership roles. But fortunately, rarely will an adult turn down a willing and able teenage volunteer. HOBY student leaders have been taught that leadership and the ability to make a positive difference through service does not require official titles. Service projects provide youth with the opportunity to use many leadership skills such as: goal setting and project scoping, verbal and written communication, active listening and appreciating the perspective of others, volunteer recruitment and team building, project planning and management, budgeting, fundraising, and money

NEW DIRECTIONS FOR STUDENT LEADERSHIP • DOI: 10.1002/yd

management, organization and delegation, research and comprehension, and success measurement and reporting.

A Leadership Development Model to Fit HOBY's Service Values

Recognizing the need to ground HOBY's programs in a theoretical framework, it became important to select the right leadership model to fit with the values of our organization and programs. For leadership development programs that have a special emphasis on service, social responsibility, the development of social change agents, or leadership for the common good, the SCM of leadership development (HERI, 1996) was a good fit. In fact, from its inception 20 years ago, the model advocated for the use of service-learning as a powerful approach to student learning and leadership development (HERI, 1996). The SCM is also the model most often claimed to be grounding collegiate leadership programs (Owen, 2012).

Table 8.2 provides a brief overview of the leadership values the model espouses. This framework now provides a roadmap for the HOBY curriculum. We find that while it does not oversimplify leadership issues, it offers students a way to assess their own leadership development, identify areas of needed growth, and facilitate their own learning—thus preparing them for a lifetime of learning from new experiences.

Social Change Model.   In 2007, HOBY began a 4-year process of implementing the use of the social change model of leadership development and service-learning methodology as a basis for Leadership Seminar and World Leadership Congress curriculum for high school sophomores. Since HOBY Leadership Seminars operate nationwide and are produced by volunteers, this was not a small undertaking. The full implementation took 4 years, culminating in spring 2010. The implementation process HOBY used will be described later in this chapter.

In 2012, HOBY embarked on developing a new program offering, the Advanced Leadership Academy (ALA), for high school juniors and seniors. Students who participate in ALA leave with a written service or social entrepreneurship project plan and a mentor to help implement their project. College credit for the program was among the goals in developing the ALA; therefore, a college textbook was needed. After an exhaustive search process, *Leadership for a Better World: Understanding the Social Change Model of Leadership Development* (Komives, Wagner & Associates, 2009) was chosen as the foundational book for the program. It brought the social change model to life in an accessible book. A team of HOBY staff and volunteers spent one year developing an accompanying curriculum that would first be used in winter 2013 for the first ALA. Since then, the curriculum has been revised and enhanced. In 2015, students were able to receive transferable college credit through a partnership with George Mason University.

NEW DIRECTIONS FOR STUDENT LEADERSHIP • DOI: 10.1002/yd

Table 8.2   The Seven C's: The Critical Values of the Social Change Model of Leadership Development

Individual Values	
Consciousness of Self	Being aware of the beliefs, values, attitudes, and emotions that motivate you to take action. Being mindful, or aware of your current emotional state, behavior, and perceptual lenses.
Congruence	Acting in ways that are consistent with your values and beliefs. Thinking, feeling, and behaving with consistency, genuineness, authenticity, and honesty toward others.
Commitment	Having significant investment in an idea or person, both in terms of intensity and duration. Having the energy to serve the group and its goals. Commitment originates from within, but others can create an environment that supports an individual's passions.
Group Values	
Collaboration	Working with others in a common effort, sharing responsibility, authority, and accountability. Multiplying group effectiveness by capitalizing on various perspectives and talents, and on the power of diversity to generate creative solutions and actions.
Common Purpose	Having shared aims and values. Involving others in building a group's vision and purpose.
Controversy with Civility	Recognizing two fundamental realities of any creative effort: (1) that differences in viewpoint are inevitable, and (2) that such differences must be aired openly but with civility.
Community Values	
Citizenship	Believing in a process whereby an individual and/or a group become responsibly connected to the community and to society through some activity. Recognizing that members of communities are not independent, but interdependent. Recognizing individuals and groups have responsibility for the welfare of others.
Since it is a key assumption of the SCM that the ultimate goal of leadership is positive social change, "**change**" is considered to be at the "hub" of the SCM.	
Change	Believing in the importance of making a better world and a better society for oneself and others. Believing that individuals, groups, and communities have the ability to work together to make that change.

(Adapted from Higher Education Research Institute, 1996, p. 21 and Tyree, 1998, p. 176.)
Source: From W. Wagner (2006). The social change model of leadership: A brief overview. *Concepts & Connections, 15*(1), 9. Used with permission from the National Clearinghouse for Leadership Programs.

The Community Leadership Workshop program for high school freshmen was then updated to reflect the methodologies in 2015. HOBY's philosophy was also adjusted slightly that "effective positive leadership is ultimately service to humanity to make the world a better place" (What Is HOBY?, 2015).

Figure 8.1.   Leadership for Service (L4S) Model

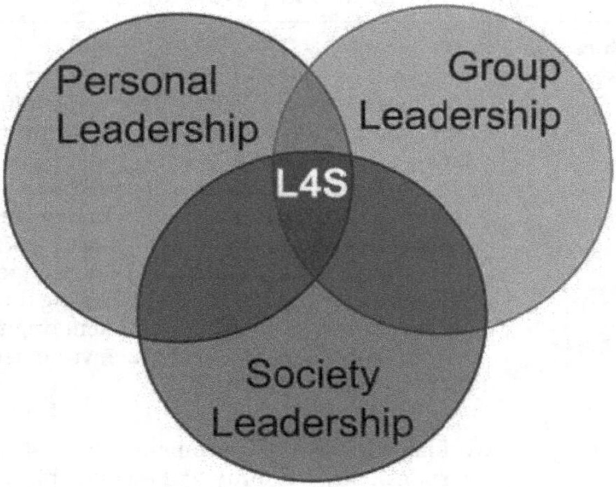

Source: Adapted from *Social Change Model of Leadership Development* (HERI, 1996).

Combining the Social Change Model with Service-Learning Methodology

The social change model frames leadership from three sets of values: individual, group, and community values (HERI, 1996). Figure 8.1 is used by HOBY to show that using all three of these perspectives simultaneously are necessary for HOBY's Leadership for Service elements. To implement a service project well, students understand they must attend to all three.

Combining the SCM with the service learning methodology for leadership education is a truly powerful experiential learning pedagogy. Figure 8.2 depicts the HOBY Active Leadership Cycle, which applies to both service and leadership, and shares several common elements with Kolb's experiential learning cycle (1983), in particular action, reflection on the experience, and the meaning-making that results in learning. By sharing this model with our program participants we are able to be explicit about the learning experience it is our goal to provide. In essence, this cycle represents the center Leadership for Service (L4S) (Leadership for Service [L4S] Challenge, 2015 http://www.hoby.org/alumni/leadership-for-service) portion of the social change model graphic.

A HOBY Program Described

HOBY programs are interactive and dynamic and all use the social change model of leadership development and service-learning methodology. Students learn theory and information, interact with adult leaders, listen to motivational speakers, participate in leadership activities and service projects,

Figure 8.2.   Leadership for Service (L4S) Cycle

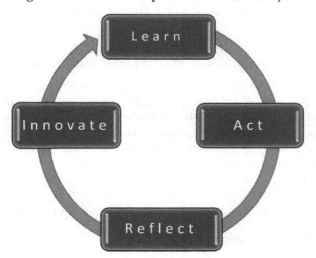

explore their own personal leadership skills, practice how they will lead a team, and consider how they can make a positive impact in their community. HOBY uses a combination of methods to facilitate learning by every young leader, including presentations, guided journaling, simulation activities, field trips, service projects, and small group facilitated discussions.

HOBY programs have become known for their high energy—and while there are enthusiastic cheers that HOBY alumni know well, there is also time for silence. There is time to speak and time for listening, time for fun activities and time for serious stillness, time for focused learning and time for social celebration, time to question and time for gratitude. There is also purposeful reflection time in the form of small group discussion facilitated by a trained adult. HOBY maintains a ratio of 12:1 or fewer for students to adults in small groups so that every student receives personalized attention and coaching.

Students who experience a HOBY program will often describe it as "life-changing." They will explain they had never experienced such an exciting and empowering learning environment, "I've never seen so many teenagers genuinely interested in volunteering, not for college credits, but to make a difference," wrote student Cassandra Hsiao in 2015 about her HOBY experience. She continued, "They [the speakers] opened our eyes to what we could accomplish and never took our age into account. They taught us the power of the ripple effect and showed us that anything is possible if we dare to embark on the outstanding journey of life. ... HOBY moved me, and I will move the world" (personal communication, 2015). Robert Baurley summed up HOBY this way, "My HOBY Leadership Seminar taught me that I have potential; the HOBY World Leadership Congress taught me that I have a place in the world; and the HOBY Advanced Leadership Academy taught me how to use my potential to change the world" (personal communication, 2015).

HOBY's Major Program Change Implementation Life Cycle

As mentioned earlier in this chapter, program implementation at HOBY is not a small undertaking due to the size, culture, and volunteer nature of the organization. HOBY has a large number of stakeholders to consider and communicate with including alumni, volunteers, staff, parents, schools, donors, and other supporters. So making a major change is more like turning a cruise ship than a speed boat, as working with all stakeholders to create buy-in takes time. Having a theoretical model to guide program changes provided a framework and language to help channel everyone's energies in one general direction. The four-year implementation plan is described below.

Year 0: Development

- Determine program initiation/change and goals
- Develop program implementation materials
- Develop program training methods and materials
- Determine number and type of pilot sites desired for limited pilot in Year 1

All stakeholders are represented in program change and goal setting exercises through a variety of advisory committees, working teams, and focus groups. The materials development for the two audiences, the volunteers who will deliver the program, as well as the students who will receive the program, is delegated to a small team of professional staff and experienced volunteers with the expertise needed to create them. Pilot sites are selected based on a number of criteria chosen to test the program change. These criteria include national geography, urban and rural programs, number of participants, and relative strength of the site.

Year 1: Limited Pilot

- Announce and publish limited pilot plan
- Select pilot sites for limited pilot
- Train pilot sites and educate volunteers on pilot purpose
- Work with pilot sites on implementation
- Develop pilot evaluation
- Collect and analyze pilot data
- Determine program revisions based on data
- Revise program implementation and training materials as necessary

Communication with all stakeholders remains important at every stage of the process. Detailed training is critical for volunteers to understand what the change is, why the change is taking place, and how to implement the change in programming. Evaluation methods and materials must be created and data collected and analyzed to determine appropriate next steps. This often takes longer than anticipated as formal recommendations are developed based on the final analysis. Once decisions are made regarding next steps, program and training materials revision is usually swift, however.

Year 2: Revision and Opt-In

- Communicate Year one pilot results
- Announce and publish open pilot plan
- Develop pilot site criteria and approve pilot sites for open pilot
- Train pilot sites and educate volunteers on pilot purpose
- Work with pilot sites to implement pilot
- Update pilot evaluation
- Collect pilot data and analyze
- Determine changes based on data
- Revise program implementation and training materials

At this stage, "selling" the program change becomes important to gain majority support for moving forward with implementation on an opt-in basis. The more people and sites that get onboard at this stage, the easier full implementation will be later. Marketing pilot success is a key message, while preparing volunteers for the challenges that should be anticipated.

Year 3: Full Implementation

- Communicate Year 2 pilot results
- Determine if organization, volunteers, and program are truly prepared for successful full implementation
- Announce and publish nationwide mandatory implementation plan
- Train sites and educate volunteers on pilot purpose
- Work with sites on implementation and integration
- Finalize all documentation
- Collect and continuously evaluate data

There will be some volunteers who will resist change until the implementation becomes mandatory. They are happy to let others do the testing and work out the kinks, but are satisfied with coming onboard at the end of the change process. There will be still others, however, that will continue to resist change even after it has been made mandatory. These folks have to be worked with individually to bring them into alignment with the rest of the organization. In a rare few cases, individuals may choose to leave the organization rather than accept the program change.

The Role of a Shared Theoretical Model and Commitment to Service-Learning in HOBY Programs

When working with a nationwide organization that utilizes over 4,000 volunteers for program delivery, a shared theoretical model creates a common foundation for the staff and volunteers developing and implementing programs, and students experiencing programs. Theory provides a consistency of messaging and desired learning outcomes in programming across geography, age, experience, and time. Both our chosen theoretical model and service-learning methodology are taught to key volunteers at HOBY's Training Institute using a train-the-trainer approach, such that those key volunteers pass along our common framework and pedagogy to other volunteers in their state.

Implementing a shared theoretical model and pedagogy in a program with a national scope was challenging, as one would expect. By using a four-year implementation timeline and educating numerous stakeholders about the SCM and service-learning, we have arrived at a national leadership development program in which all volunteers, educators, and participants share the same leadership philosophy and community-engagement values.

References

Day, D. V., & Lance, C. E. (2004). Understanding the development of leadership complexity through latent growth modeling. In D. V. Day, S. J. Zaccaro, & S. M. Halpin (Eds.), *Leader development for transforming organizations: Growing leaders for tomorrow* (pp. 41–69). Mahwah, NJ: Erlbaum.

Day, D. V., Harrison, M. M., & Halpin, S. M. (2009). *An integrative approach to leader development: Connecting adult development, identity, and expertise.* New York, NY: Routledge.

Dugan, J. P., & Komives, S. R. (2011). Leadership theories. In S. R. Komives, J. P. Dugan, J. E. Owen, C. Slack, & W. Wagner (Eds.), *Handbook for student leadership programs.* A publication of the National Clearinghouse for Leadership Programs (pp. 35–58). San Francisco, CA: Jossey-Bass.

Dugan, J. P., & Owen, J. E. (2007). Practicing what we preach: An institutional approach to student leadership development. *The Leadership Exchange, 5*(2), 20–23.

Eich, D. (2008). A grounded theory of high-quality leadership programs: Perspectives from student leadership development programs in higher education. *Journal of Leadership & Organizational Studies, 15,* 176–187.

Halpern, D. F. (2004). The development of adult cognition: Understanding constancy and change in adult learning. In D. V. Day, S. J. Zaccaro, & S. M. Halpin (Eds.), *Leader development for transforming organizations: Growing leaders for tomorrow* (pp. 125–152). Mahwah, NJ: Erlbaum.

Higher Education Research Institute. (1996). *A social change model of leadership development (Version III).* Los Angeles: University of California Los Angeles, Higher Education Research Institute.

Kegan, R., & Lahey, L. L. (2009). *Immunity to change.* Boston, MA: Harvard Business School.

Kolb, D. A. (1983). *Experiential learning: Experience as the source of learning and development*. New York, NY: Prentice-Hall.

Komives, S. R., & Dugan, J. P. (2014). Student leadership development: Theory, research, and practice. In D. Day (Ed.), *The Oxford handbook of leadership and organizations* (pp. 805–831). New York, NY: Oxford University Press.

Komives, S. R., Wagner, W., & Associates. (2009). *Leadership for a better world: Understanding the social change model of leadership development*. San Francisco, CA: Jossey-Bass.

Leadership for Service (L4S) Challenge (2015). In *hoby.org*. Retrieved from http://www.hoby.org/alumni/leadership-for-service

Owen, J. E. (2012). *Findings from the multi-institutional study of leadership institutional survey: A national report*. College Park, MD: National Clearinghouse for Leadership Programs.

Owen, J. E. (2008). *Towards an empirical typology of collegiate leadership development programs: Examining effects on student self-efficacy and leadership for social change*. Unpublished doctoral dissertation, University of Maryland–College Park, College Park, MD.

Posner, B. Z. (2004). A leadership development instrument for students: Updated. *Journal of College Student Development*, 45, 443–456.

Wagner, W. (2006). The social change model of leadership: A brief overview. *Concepts & Connections*, 15(1), 9. Used with permission from the National Clearinghouse for Leadership Programs.

Wagner, W. (2011). Considerations of student development in leadership. In S. R. Komives, J. P. Dugan, J. E. Owen, C. Slack, & W. Wagner (Eds.), *Handbook for student leadership programs*. A publication of the National Clearinghouse for Leadership Programs (pp. 85–108). San Francisco, CA: Jossey-Bass.

Walke, J. M., (2010). *Hugh O'Brian Youth Leadership—HOBY: The first fifty years*. Virginia Beach, VA: The Donning Company.

What Is HOBY? (2015). In *hoby.org*. Retrieved from http://www.hoby.org/about/what-is-hoby

VICKI FERRENCE RAY *is the senior director of programs, Hugh O'Brian Youth Leadership (HOBY), www.hoby.org, and PhD Candidate in Administration and Leadership Studies, Indiana University of Pennsylvania.*

NEW DIRECTIONS FOR STUDENT LEADERSHIP • DOI: 10.1002/yd

Index

NEW DIRECTIONS FOR STUDENT LEADERSHIP

ORDER FORM SUBSCRIPTION AND SINGLE ISSUES

DISCOUNTED BACK ISSUES:

Use this form to receive 20% off all back issues of *New Directions for Student Leadership*.
All single issues priced at **$23.20** (normally $29.00)

TITLE	ISSUE NO.	ISBN

Call 1-800-835-6770 or see mailing instructions below. When calling, mention the promotional code JBNND to receive your discount. For a complete list of issues, please visit www.wiley.com/WileyCDA/WileyTitle/productCd-YD.html

SUBSCRIPTIONS: (1 YEAR, 4 ISSUES)

☐ New Order   ☐ Renewal

U.S.	☐ Individual: $89	☐ Institutional: $363
CANADA/MEXICO	☐ Individual: $89	☐ Institutional: $405
ALL OTHERS	☐ Individual: $113	☐ Institutional: $441

Call 1-800-835-6770 or see mailing and pricing instructions below.
Online subscriptions are available at www.onlinelibrary.wiley.com

ORDER TOTALS:

Issue / Subscription Amount: $ _____

Shipping Amount: $ _____
(for single issues only – subscription prices include shipping)

Total Amount: $ _____

SHIPPING CHARGES:
First Item $6.00
Each Add'l Item $2.00

(No sales tax for U.S. subscriptions. Canadian residents, add GST for subscription orders. Individual rate subscriptions must be paid by personal check or credit card. Individual rate subscriptions may not be resold as library copies.)

BILLING & SHIPPING INFORMATION:

☐ **PAYMENT ENCLOSED:** *(U.S. check or money order only. All payments must be in U.S. dollars.)*

☐ **CREDIT CARD:**   ☐ VISA   ☐ MC   ☐ AMEX

Card number _____ Exp. Date _____

Card Holder Name _____ Card Issue # _____

Signature _____ Day Phone _____

☐ **BILL ME:** *(U.S. institutional orders only. Purchase order required.)*

Purchase order # _____
Federal Tax ID 13559302 • GST 89102-8052

Name _____

Address _____

Phone _____ E-mail _____

Copy or detach page and send to: **John Wiley & Sons, Inc. / Jossey Bass**
PO Box 55381
Boston, MA 02205-9850

PROMO JBNND